Maine Real Estate Law and Rule Handbook

2019 Edition

Edited By Walter Boomsma

Published by
Abbot Village Press
17 River Road
Abbot ME 04406 USA
Portions copyright 2020 by Walter Boomsma

First edition January 2020

Some illustrations licensed by Presenter Media
PresenterMedia.com
4416 S. Technology Drive
Sioux Falls SD 57106 USA

ISBN: 978-1-950945-02-3

Printed in the United States of America

PREFACE

I decided to develop this handbook after several years of using various versions in the pre-licensing courses I teach. Students have expressed a desire for something more "user friendly."

In an effort to achieve this, I have considered content and context. In terms of content, I have created a fairly detailed "Table of Contents" that will allow students and licensees to quickly locate information. I have also eliminated some references, including sections that have been repealed. No changes were made to any text, but some formatting was adjusted solely for the sake of clarity and some consistency. My intent was to create an educational tool more than a legal reference book.

A legal handbook should include a little humor.

One important point for students to remember is when researching a particular question or topic it is necessary to look beyond the obvious and avoid quickly drawing a conclusion based on one statute or rule. One must always consider the full body of the laws and rules, understanding that a given topic may be referenced more than once.

The easiest way to refer to the latest versions of statutes is to visit the following website:

http://www.mainelegislature.org/legis/statutes/

Note that the phrase "is current through December 25, 2019" refers only to statutes. Rules are not governed by a single date, but the rules included are current through that same date.

The Maine Real Estate Commission is part of the Department of Business Regulation and Office of Licensing and Regulation. Title 5, Title 10, and the Office of Licensing and Regulation Rules refer to this umbrella and licensing in general

This handbook includes:

- MRS Title 32, Chapter 114: Real Estate Brokerage License Act

- MRS Title 32, Chapter 124: Real Estate Appraisal
  (Portion only as applies to appraisals and opinions of value)

- Maine Real Estate Commission Rules

The following pertain to licensing in general:

- MRS Title 5, Chapter 341: Occupational License Disqualification

- MRS Title 10, Chapter 901: Department of Professional Regulation

- Portions of the Office of Licensing and Registration Rules

TABLE OF CONTENTS

CONTENTS

MAINE REVISED STATUTE TITLE 32 CHAPTER 114
REAL ESTATE BROKERAGE LICENSE ACT

Subchapter 1: General Provisions

§13001 DEFINITIONS

As used in this chapter, unless the context otherwise indicates, the following terms have the following meanings:

1. **Real estate.** "Real estate" means all estates and lesser interests in land and an existing business if real estate is a part of the business

1-A Commission. "Commission" means the Real Estate Commission.

1-B Director. "Director" means the director of the Real Estate Commission.

2. **Real estate Brokerage.** "Real estate brokerage" means a single instance of offering, attempting to conduct or conducting services on behalf of another for compensation, or with the expectation of receiving compensation, calculated to result in the transfer of an interest in real estate. Real estate brokerage includes, but is not limited to, the following activities conducted in behalf of another:
   A. Listing real estate for sale or exchange;
   B. Promoting the purchase, sale or exchange of real estate;
   C. Procuring of prospects calculated to result in the purchase, sale or exchange of real estate;
   D. Advertising or holding oneself out as offering any services described in this subsection;
   E. Negotiating the purchase, sale or exchange of real estate;
   F. Buying options on real estate or selling real estate options or the real estate under option;
   G. Acting as a finder to facilitate the purchase, sale or exchange of real estate; and
   H. Buying, selling or exchanging real estate.

§13002 EXCEPTIONS TO BROKERAGE

Real estate brokerage does not include the following:

1. **Transactions by owner or lessor.** Transactions conducted by any person who is the owner or lessor of the real estate, or to their regular employees with regard to the employer's real estate, provided that:

A. The real estate transaction services rendered by the employee are performed as an incident to the usual duties performed for the employer; or

B. The real estate transaction services are subject to the provisions of the Maine Condominium Act, Title 33, chapter 31;

2. Transactions by attorneys-at-law. Transactions conducted by an attorney-at-law in the performance of duties as an attorney-at-law. This exception does not apply to attorneys who are regularly engaged in real estate brokerage;

3. Exception. Any person licensed as an auctioneer under chapter 5, hired to call bids at an auction, if the person employed does not prepare contracts or otherwise control the actual sale or take custody of any part of the purchase price; and

4. Time share. Real estate transaction services subject to the provisions of Title 33, chapter 10-A.

§13003. LICENSE REQUIRED

It is unlawful for any person or entity to engage in real estate brokerage without a current real estate brokerage agency license issued under this chapter or a license authorizing the person to engage in brokerage activity on behalf of a brokerage agency.

§13004. CIVIL ACTIONS

No person or entity may bring or maintain any action in the courts of this State for the collection of compensation for real estate brokerage services, without first proving that the person or entity was properly licensed by the Real Estate Commission at the time the cause of action arose.

§13005. PENALTIES

A person or entity who violates any provision of this chapter commits a civil violation for which a forfeiture of not more than $2,000 for each violation may be adjudged, plus the amount of compensation received in the subject transaction. Any officer or agent of an entity who personally participates in or is accessory to a violation of this chapter is subject to the penalties prescribed under this section. Any court of competent jurisdiction has full power to try any violation of this chapter and, upon conviction, the court may at its discretion revoke or suspend the license of the person or entity so convicted. All fines and penalties over and above the cost of court proceedings inure to the commission. A violation of this chapter includes performing or attempting to perform those acts that constitute prohibited practices. The State may bring an action in Superior Court to enjoin any person from violating this chapter, regardless of whether other administrative, civil or criminal proceedings have been or may be instituted.

§13006. CONFIDENTIALITY

All hearings and records of hearings conducted by the grievance committee or the professional standards committee of any state or regional professional real estate association or board are confidential and are exempt from discovery.

§13007. FEES

The Director of the Office of Licensing and Registration within the Department of Professional and Financial Regulation may establish by rule fees for purposes authorized under this chapter in amounts that are reasonable and necessary for their respective purposes, except that the fee for any one purpose may not exceed $100. Rules adopted pursuant to this section are routine technical rules pursuant to Title 5, chapter 375, subchapter 2-A.

Subchapter 2: COMMISSION

§13061. DECLARATION OF POLICY

It is declared to be the policy of the State that licensees shall be supervised by the Real Estate Commission in a manner to ensure that they meet standards which will promote public understanding and confidence in the business of real estate brokerage.

§13062. REAL ESTATE COMMISSION; ORGANIZATION

1. **Real Estate Commission composition.** The Real Estate Commission, established by Title 5, section 12004-A, subsection 37, consists of 4 industry members and 2 public members as defined in Title 5, section 12004-A.
2. **Qualifications.** Each industry member of the commission must have been a real estate broker or associate broker by vocation in this State for at least 5 years prior to appointment.
3. **Geographic distribution.**
4. **Terms; removal.** Terms of the members of the commission are for 3 years. Members may be removed by the Governor for cause.
5. **Quorum; procedure.** Four members of the commission constitute a quorum .

6. **Appointments.** The members of the commission are appointed by the Governor. Appointments of members must comply with Title 10, section 8009.

7. **Chair.** The commission shall annually elect a chair from its members.

§13065. RULES

The commission may establish guidelines and rules by which this chapter shall be administered. Rules shall be subject to the Maine Administrative Procedure Act, Title 5, chapter 375, subchapter II and consistent with the law to govern the following:

1. **Adjudicatory hearings.**

2. **Investigations.**

3. **Brokerage practice.** The commission may adopt rules consistent with the standards set forth in this chapter governing real estate brokerage practices in order to establish standards of practice which serve the interests of both the public and the industry.

4. **License qualifications.** The commission may adopt rules relating to the qualifications and application for any license authorized under this chapter as are deemed necessary to assure that applicants are sufficiently trustworthy and competent to transact the business for which they will be licensed.

5. **Fees.**

6. **Education.** The commission may adopt rules to be applied in determining whether educational programs meet the license qualifications required under this chapter.

7. **Supervision of employees.** The commission shall adopt rules defining the authority and responsibility of designated brokers in supervising sales agents, as well as other brokerage related employees and independent contractors.

8. **Other.** The commission may adopt and enforce such other rules as are necessary for the performance of its duties under this chapter.

§13067-A. DENIAL OR REFUSAL TO RENEW LICENSE; DISCIPLINARY ACTION

In addition to the grounds enumerated in Title 10, section 8003, subsection 5-A, paragraph A, the commission may deny a license, refuse to renew a license or impose the disciplinary sanctions authorized by Title 10, section 8003, subsection 5-A for:

1 **Lack of trustworthiness.** Lack of trustworthiness and competence to transact real estate brokerage
services in such manner as to safeguard the interests of the public;

2. **Misconduct.** Any act or conduct, whether of the same or different character than specified in this chapter, that constitutes or demonstrates bad faith, incompetency, untrustworthiness or dishonest, fraudulent or improper dealings;

3. **Act that constitutes grounds for denial.** Performing or attempting to perform any act or acts for which a license may lawfully be denied to any applicant;

4. **Substantial misrepresentation.** Making any substantial misrepresentation by omission or commission, but not including innocent misrepresentation;

5. **Failure to protect principal.** Failing to act in a reasonably prudent manner in order to protect and promote the interests of the principal with absolute fidelity;

6. **Failure to avoid error, exaggeration or concealment.** Failing to act in a reasonably prudent manner in order to avoid error, exaggeration or concealment of pertinent information;

7. **Liability of agency and designated broker.** Violation of this chapter by a licensed or unlicensed person acting on the agency's behalf if:

   A. The designated broker had prior knowledge and did not take reasonable action to prevent the violation;

   B. The designated broker permitted or authorized a person to engage in activity for which that person was not properly licensed; or

   C. The designated broker failed to exercise a reasonable degree of supervision over employees and independent contractors commensurate with their qualifications and experience;

8. **Unlawful payment.** Offering, promising, allowing, giving or paying, directly or indirectly, any part or share of compensation arising or accruing from a real estate brokerage transaction to any person who is not licensed to perform the service for which the person is or would be compensated, if a license is required under this chapter for performance of that service. A licensee may not be employed by or accept brokerage compensation from any person other than the agency under which the licensee is at the time licensed. An agency may share compensation with a nonresident

licensee when the service by the nonresident is performed outside this State;

9. **Suspension or revocation of license.** Having had a professional or occupational license application rejected for reasons related to untrustworthiness within 3 years prior to the date of application or had a professional or occupational license suspended or revoked for disciplinary reasons; and

10. **Failure to meet professional qualifications; failure to submit complete application.** Failing to meet the professional qualifications for licensure as provided in this subchapter or failing to submit a complete application within 30 days after being notified of the materials needed to complete the application.

§13069. DIRECTOR

1. **Appointment.** The Commissioner of Professional and Financial Regulation, with the advice of the Real Estate Commission and subject to the Civil Service Law, shall appoint a director of the commission.

2. **Duties.** The director is responsible for the management of the commission's affairs, within the guidelines, policies and rules established by the commission and for carrying out the duties allocated to the director under this chapter. Duties of the director may be carried out by the director's designee, other than a member of the commission.

3. **Employees.**

4. **Disposal of fees; expenses.**

4-A. **Real estate account.**

5. **Advocate.** The director shall seek to protect the interests of the public and the industry in the administration of this chapter. In this capacity, the director may serve as an advocate in any proceeding before the commission, presenting evidence and argument in support of a recommended disposition.

6. **Investigations.** The director may investigate the actions of any licensee under this chapter, or any person or entity who assumes to act in a capacity requiring a license under this chapter, upon receipt of a verified written complaint or in accordance with the guidelines prescribed by commission rule. Upon completion of the investigation, the director shall take one of the following actions:

   A. With the commission's approval, dismiss the complaint;

   B. With the consent of the parties and subject to approval of the commission and commission counsel, execute a consent agreement; or

   C. Issue a staff petition for hearing before the commission, which may include a recommended disposition.

7. **Subpoenas.** The director may issue subpoenas to compel the attendance of witnesses at hearings and to compel the production of documents and other records deemed necessary in connection with the administration of this chapter. Whenever a person refuses to obey a subpoena duly issued by the director, the Superior Court for Kennebec County or any court of this State, within the jurisdiction of which the person resides or transacts business, shall have jurisdiction to issue to that person an order requiring him to comply with the subpoena and any failure to obey that order may be punished by the court as contempt. Refusal to obey the director's subpoena also constitutes a violation of this chapter

8. **Denial of licenses.** The director may only issue a license to persons or entities meeting the requirements of this chapter. If it appears to the director that grounds for denial of a license or renewal exists, the director shall deny the license or renewal and notify the applicant in writing of the basis for denial together with notice of the applicant's right to a hearing before the commission, if requested in accordance with commission rules within a 30-day period. The director shall not issue a license to any applicant for renewal if the license has been expired for more than 90 days, unless the applicant passes the license examination designated by commission rule for this purpose.

Subchapter 3: REAL ESTATE BROKERAGE AGENCY

§13171. REAL ESTATE BROKERAGE AGENCY

As used in this chapter, except for subchapter 7, "real estate brokerage agency" or "agency" means any person or entity engaged in real estate brokerage services through its designated broker, associates or employees and licensed by the commission as a real estate brokerage agency.

§13172. ORIGINAL APPLICATION

Each applicant for an original agency license shall submit an application, signed by the authorized agency official, together with the fee as set under section 13007.

§13173. AGENCY LICENSE QUALIFICATIONS

1. **Designated broker.** The owner or a duly authorized agency official shall hold a Maine real estate broker license and be designated by the agency to act for it in the conduct of real estate brokerage.
2. **Employees.** Every person employed by or on behalf of the agency in the performance of real estate brokerage shall be properly licensed under this chapter.
3. **Reputation.** The agency and its owner or principal officers, if previously engaged in any business, shall bear a good reputation for honesty, truthfulness, fair dealing and competency.
4. **Nonresidents.** The following applies to nonresidents.
   A. Nonresident applicants shall hold a similar license in good standing and maintain an active place of business in its resident jurisdiction.
5. **Place of business.** Every agency holding an active license shall maintain a fixed and definite place of business where its designated broker and employees may be personally contacted without unreasonable delay.
6. **Branch office.** Other locations that are advertised as locations where the public may contact the agency or its employees concerning brokerage services must be licensed as a branch office.

§13174. LICENSE DENIAL

A license may be denied to any agency applicant:

1. **Complete and accurate application.** Who fails to submit a complete and accurate application;
2. **Proof of qualifications.** Who fails to submit satisfactory proof that it has met the qualifications specified in this chapter and is sufficiently trustworthy and competent to transact real estate brokerage services in such a manner as to safeguard the interests of the public;
3. **Conviction of crime.** Subject to Title 5, chapter 341, if the owner or principal entity officials have been convicted of any Class A, B or C crime or any crime which bears directly on the practice of real estate brokerage; or
4. **Revocation of license.** If the agency and its owner or its principal officers have had any professional or occupational license revoked for disciplinary reasons, or an application rejected for reasons relating to untrustworthiness, within 3 years prior to the date of application.

§13175. AGENCY CHANGES

Any change of address, name or other material changes in the conditions or qualifications set forth in the original application must be reported to the director no later than 10 days after the change. Upon application and payment of the fee as set under section 13007, the commission records must be changed and a new license must be issued for the unexpired term of the current license, if appropriate.

§13176. TRADE NAMES

Agencies may conduct business under a trade name, provided that their license is issued under the trade name. If an agency is licensed with a trade name, that trade name shall be used by the agency, its employees and independent contractors in all real estate brokerage related advertising. The director may refuse to issue a license under a specific trade name if the name is deemed to be misleading, deceptive or will likely result in confusion with other existing businesses.

§13177-A. BROKERAGE AGREEMENTS

1. **Definitions.** As used in this section, "brokerage agreement," "real estate brokerage agency" and "client" have the same meanings as in section 13271.
2. **Written agreements.** A brokerage agreement between a real estate brokerage agency and a client must be in writing and, at a minimum, include the following:
   A. The signature of the client to be charged;
   B. The terms and conditions of the brokerage services to be provided;
   C. The method or amount of compensation to be paid;
   D. The date upon which the agreement will expire; and
   E. A statement that the agreement creates an agency-client relationship.

A brokerage agreement may not be enforced against any client who in good faith subsequently engages the services of another real estate brokerage agency following the expiration date of the first brokerage agreement. Any brokerage agreement provision extending a real estate brokerage agency's right to a fee following expiration of the brokerage agreement may not extend that right beyond 6 months

§13178. TRUST ACCOUNTS

Every agency shall maintain a federally insured account or accounts in a financial institution authorized to do business in this State, as defined in Title 9-B, section 131, subsection 17-A, or a credit union authorized to do business in this State, as defined in Title 9-B, section 131, subsection 12-A, for the sole purpose of depositing all earnest money deposits and all other money held by it as an agency in which its clients or other persons with whom it is dealing have an interest. The trust account and withdrawal orders, including all checks drawn on the account, must name the subject agency and be identified as a real estate trust account. Real estate trust accounts must be free from trustee process, except by those persons for whom the brokerage agency has made the deposits and then only to the extent of the interest. The designated broker, except for an amount necessary to maintain the accounts not to exceed an amount prescribed by commission rule, shall withdraw from the accounts all fees due within 30 days after but not until consummation or termination of the transaction when the designated broker makes or causes to be made a full accounting to the broker's principal. The designated broker shall maintain trust accounts and supporting records in a manner prescribed by commission rule. These accounts and records must be open for inspection by the director or the director's authorized representative at the agency's place of business during generally recognized business hours. Upon order of the director, the designated broker shall authorize the director in writing to confirm the balance of funds held in all agency trust accounts. Rules adopted pursuant to this section are routine technical rules as defined in Title 5, chapter 375, subchapter 2-A.

§13179. SUPERVISION OF EMPLOYEES

The designated broker shall exercise a reasonable level of supervision commensurate with the level of qualification and experience of agency employees and independent contractors supervised, in order to protect and promote the interests of its clients with absolute fidelity. The designated broker shall not permit or authorize any person to engage in any activity for which they are not properly licensed.

§13180. TERMINATION OF EMPLOYMENT

When any broker, associate broker or real estate sales agent is discharged or terminates employment with a brokerage agency, the designated broker shall immediately send a communication to the last known address of the broker, associate broker or sales agent advising the broker, associate broker or sales agent that the commission has been notified. The designated broker shall deliver a copy of the communication to the commission.

Upon receipt of the notice of termination by the licensee, the license is void and may only be reinstated or placed on inactive status after proper application and payment of the prescribed fee. It is unlawful for any broker, associate broker or real estate sales agent to perform any brokerage services without first receiving a new active license.

§13181. CONTENTS; DISPLAY

The director shall issue to each agency a license in the form and size prescribed by the Commissioner of Professional and Financial Regulation. The license of each broker, associate broker and sales agent must be delivered or mailed to the designated broker and be kept in the custody and control of the designated broker. It is the duty of the designated broker to conspicuously display the agency license in the broker's place of business.

§13182. AGENCY LICENSE RENEWAL

Agency licenses expire on December 3 1st, or at such times as the Commissioner of Professional and Financial Regulation may designate, of each biennial period for which it was issued. Upon application and payment of the fee as set under section 13007, a renewal license is issued for each ensuing biennial period in the absence of any reason or condition that might warrant denial of a license. The suspension, revocation or expiration of an agency or designated broker's license automatically voids every license granted to any person by virtue of the person's employment by the agency whose license has been suspended, revoked or expired pending a change of employer and the issuance of a new license. The new license is issued without charge if granted during the same biennial period in which the original was granted.

§13183. ACTS AUTHORIZED

An agency, through its designated broker, may perform all of the brokerage services contemplated by this chapter and may employ or retain others to perform brokerage services on behalf of the agency. The designated broker may also delegate any of the designated broker's duties and authority provided for under this chapter to an agency affiliate, but when doing so is not relieved of any responsibility imposed by this chapter.

§13184. REAL ESTATE BROKERAGE RECORDS; RETENTION

A designated broker shall maintain complete and adequate records of all real estate brokerage activity conducted on behalf of the broker's agency. The commission shall specify by rule the records required to establish complete and adequate records, including retention schedules. The records must be open for inspection by the director or the director's authorized representative at the agency's place of business during generally recognized business hours.

Subchapter 4: BROKERS, ASSOCIATE BROKERS, SALES AGENTS AND TIMESHARE AGENTS:

§13191. GENERAL QUALIFICATIONS
1. **Application.** Applicants must submit an application together with the fee as set under section 13007.
2. **Age.** The applicant shall have reached his 18th birthday at the time of his application.
3. **Residence.** The applicant shall provide evidence of his legal residence.
4. **High school.** The applicant shall be a high school graduate or hold an equivalency certificate.
5. **Reputation.** The applicant must have a good reputation for honesty, truthfulness, fair dealing and competency.
6. **Active license.** Upon application for an active license, the applicant shall provide a written statement from the designated broker of the agency, who will be employing the applicant, authorizing issuance of the applicant's license under the agency.
7. **Single license.** No more than one license may be issued to any person for the same period of time. In the event of a change in an employer, another license shall not be issued until the current license has been returned or for which a satisfactory accounting has been made.

§13193. NONRESIDENTS
In lieu of education and experience requirements, nonresident original license applicants must hold a similar active license in good standing in another jurisdiction and must appear at such time and place as the director may designate for the purpose of written examination pertaining to Maine real estate laws.

§13194. LICENSE RENEWAL
Licenses expire on December 31st, or at such other times as the Commissioner of Professional and Financial Regulation may designate, of each biennial period for which it was issued, except those licenses issued under section 13200. The director shall issue a renewal license for each ensuing biennial period in the absence of any reason or condition that might warrant the refusal of granting a license, upon receipt of the

written request of the applicant, the biennial fee as set under section 13007 for the license and upon the applicant presenting evidence of compliance with the requirements of section 13197. The director shall deny a renewal license to any applicant whose license has lapsed for more than 90 days, unless the renewal license applicant passes the license examination designated by commission rule for this purpose.

§13195. CHANGES

Any change of address, name or other material change in the conditions or qualifications set forth in the original application, including but not limited to criminal convictions or suspension or revocation of any professional license, must be reported to the director no later than 10 days after the change. Upon application and payment of the fee as set under section 13007, the commission records must be changed and a new license issued for the unexpired term of the current license, if appropriate.

§13196. INACTIVE LICENSES

1. **Placement on inactive status.** Any licensee who does not desire to perform any of the activities described in section 13001 and who wants to preserve the license while not engaged in any brokerage activity may apply to the commission for inactive status upon payment of the fee as set under section 13007. The commission may place the license on inactive status and issue an inactive license only upon application by the licensee. During inactive status, the licensee is required to renew the license biennially, but is not required to maintain a place of business or meet the educational provisions of section 13197.

2. **Reinstatement to active status.** Licensees who have remained on inactive status for 6 years or more may have their licenses reinstated to active status by submitting an application and fee and by successfully passing a license examination designated by commission rule for this purpose. Licensees who activate within 6 years of the initial inactive license may activate by successfully completing the designated examination or by completing continuing education courses that meet commission approved clock hours as follows:

    A. For those applicants remaining inactive from the issuance of the inactive licenses up to 2 years, 21 clock hours of continuing education completed within the previous biennium;

B. For those applicants remaining inactive for more than 2 years but less than 4 years, 28 clock hours of continuing education completed within the previous biennium; or

C. For those applicants remaining inactive for more than 4 years but less than 6 years, 36 clock hours of continuing education completed within the previous biennium.

§13197. CONTINUING EDUCATION

1. **Requirement.** As a prerequisite to renewal of a license, applicants must complete 21 clock hours of continuing education within 2 years prior to the date of application in programs or courses approved by the commission. This requirement does not apply to agency and company licenses.

2. **Program approval.** Each application for approval of a continuing education program must be submitted according to the guidelines prescribed by the commission, together with the fee as set under section 13007. The fee is retained whether or not the application is approved, except that the commission may waive the application fee for any program or course for the purpose of promoting the intent of this section and that meets the standards prescribed by rule.

3. **Core requirement.** The commission may establish a core educational requirement for each license type, not to exceed 6 clock hours, in which case the remaining requirement shall be fulfilled from elective programs approved by the commission.

4. **Voluntary certification program.** The commission may establish a program for recognizing real estate brokers who have advanced education, training and experience in a specialized discipline related to the field of real estate. Standards to be met in order to be certified shall be prescribed by rules adopted by the commission, subject to the Maine Administrative Procedure Act, Title 5, chapter 375.

§13198. REAL ESTATE BROKER

1. **Definition**. "Real estate broker" or "broker" means any person employed by or on behalf of an agency to perform brokerage and licensed by the commission as a broker.

2. **Professional qualifications.** An applicant for a broker license must meet the qualifications under paragraphs A and B.

A. The applicant must have been licensed as an associate broker affiliated with a real estate brokerage agency for 2 years within the 5 years immediately preceding the date of application.

B. The applicant must satisfactorily complete the course of study meeting guidelines established by the commission.

3. **Acts authorized.** Each broker license granted entitles the holder to perform all of the acts contemplated under this chapter on behalf of an agency, including being designated by the agency to act for it.

§13199. ASSOCIATE REAL ESTATE BROKER

1. **Definition.** "Associate real estate broker" or "associate broker" means any person employed by or on behalf of an agency to perform real estate brokerage services and licensed by the commission as an associate broker.

2. **Professional qualifications.**

2-A. **Professional qualifications.** An applicant for an associate broker license must have practiced as a real estate sales agent for 2 years within the 5 years immediately preceding the date of application and satisfactorily completed a course of study meeting guidelines established by the commission. The commission may not issue a license under this section until an individual has completed 2 years as a licensed real estate sales agent.

3. **Acts authorized.** Each associate broker license granted entitles the holder to perform all of the acts contemplated by this chapter, on behalf of an agency.

§13200. REAL ESTATE SALES AGENT

1. **Definition.** "Real estate sales agent" or "sales agent" means any person employed by or on behalf of an agency to perform real estate brokerage services in a training capacity and licensed by the commission as a sales agent.

2. **Professional qualification.** Each applicant for a sales agent license must meet the following qualifications:

   A. The applicant must satisfactorily complete a course of study meeting commission established guidelines; and

   B. The applicant must appear at such time and place as the director may designate for the purpose of a written sales agent examination.

3. **Acts authorized.** Each sales agent license granted shall entitle the holder to perform all brokerage services contemplated by this chapter which are specifically authorized by the designated broker and which are within the guidelines established by the commission for sales agents.

4. **License term.** Sales agent licenses shall be issued for 2 years and may not be renewed. A new sales agent license may not be reissued within 5 years following the date the previous sales agent license was issued.

5. **Waiver.** The commission may grant waivers to allow individuals to remain licensed as sales agents beyond the 2-year term specified in subsection 4. Waivers shall be granted on the basis of extenuating circumstances as defined by rules promulgated by the commission.

Subchapter 6: OPINIONS OF VALUE

§13251-A. CONFLICT OF INTEREST

A real estate broker or associate broker may not knowingly provide or offer an appraisal or opinion of market value, as set forth in section 14004, on real estate in a transaction where the broker or associate broker, or any other licensee licensed with the agency, is to receive a fee on that transaction.

Subchapter 7: REAL ESTATE BROKERAGE RELATIONSHIPS

§13271. DEFINITIONS

As used in this subchapter, unless the context otherwise indicates, the following terms have the following meanings.

1. **Affiliated licensee.** "Affiliated licensee" means a licensee who is authorized to engage in brokerage activity by and on behalf of a real estate brokerage agency.

2. **Appointed agent.** "Appointed agent" means that affiliated licensee who is appointed by the designated broker of the affiliated licensee's real estate brokerage agency to act solely for a client of that real estate brokerage agency to the exclusion of other affiliated licensees of that real estate brokerage agency.

3. **Brokerage agreement.** "Brokerage agreement" means a contract that establishes the relationships between the parties and the brokerage services to be performed.

4. **Buyer agent.** "Buyer agent" means a real estate brokerage agency that has entered into a written brokerage agreement with the buyer in a real estate transaction to represent the buyer as its client.

5. **Client.** "Client" means a person who has entered into a written brokerage agreement with a real estate brokerage agency that has agreed to represent that person and be bound by the duties set forth in section 13272 on behalf of that person.

6. **Designated broker.** "Designated broker" means a broker designated by a real estate brokerage agency to act for the real estate brokerage agency in the conduct of real estate brokerage.

7. **Disclosed dual agent.** "Disclosed dual agent" means a real estate brokerage agency representing 2 or more clients whose interests are adverse in the same transaction with the knowledge and informed consent of the clients.

8. **Material fact.** "Material fact" means a fact that relates to the transaction and is so substantial and important as to influence the client to whom it is imparted.

9. **Ministerial acts.** "Ministerial acts" means those acts that a real estate brokerage agency performs for a person who is not a client and that are informative or clerical in nature and do not rise to the level of active representation on behalf of the person.

10. **Real estate brokerage agency**. "Real estate brokerage agency" means a person or entity providing real estate brokerage services through that person's designated broker, affiliated licensees, associates or employees and licensed by the commission as a real estate brokerage agency.

11. **Seller agent.** "Seller agent" means a real estate brokerage agency that has entered into a written brokerage agreement with the seller in a real estate transaction to represent the seller as the real estate brokerage agency's client.

12. **Subagent.** "Subagent" means a real estate brokerage agency engaged by another real estate brokerage agency to perform brokerage tasks for a client.

13. **Third party.**

13-A. **Transaction broker.** "Transaction broker" means a real estate brokerage agency that provides real estate brokerage services to one or more parties in a real estate transaction without a fiduciary relationship as a buyer agent, a seller agent, a subagent or a disclosed dual agent.

14. **Undisclosed dual agent.** "Undisclosed dual agent" means a real estate brokerage agency representing 2 or more clients whose interests are adverse in the same transaction without the knowledge and informed consent of the clients.

§13272. SCOPE OF AGENCY

A real estate brokerage agency that provides services through a brokerage agreement for a client is bound by the duties of loyalty, obedience, disclosure, confidentiality, reasonable care, diligence and accounting as set forth in this chapter. Such a real estate brokerage agency may be a seller agent, a buyer agent, a subagent or a disclosed dual agent.

§13273. SELLER AGENT

1. Duty to seller. A seller agent:

A. Shall perform the terms of the brokerage agreement made with the seller;

B. Shall promote the interests of the seller by exercising agency duties as set forth in section 13272 including:

   (1) Seeking a sale at the price and terms stated in the brokerage agreement or at a price and terms acceptable to the seller except that the seller agent is not obligated to seek additional offers to purchase the property while the property is subject to a contract of sale unless the brokerage agreement so provides;

   (2) Presenting in a timely manner all offers to and from the seller, even when the property is subject to a contract of sale;

   (3) Disclosing to the seller material facts of which the seller agent has actual knowledge or if acting in a reasonable manner should have known concerning the transaction, except as directed in section 13280;

   (4) Advising the seller to obtain expert advice on material matters that are beyond the expertise of the seller agent; and

   (5) Accounting in a timely manner for all money and property received in which the seller has or may have an interest;

C. Shall exercise reasonable skill and care;

D. Shall comply with all requirements of the laws governing real estate commission brokerage licenses and any rules adopted by the commission;

E. Shall comply with any applicable federal, state or local laws, rules, regulations or ordinances related to real estate brokerage including fair housing and civil rights laws or regulations;

F. Has an obligation to preserve confidential information provided by the seller during the course of the relationship that might have a negative impact on the seller's real estate activity unless:

   (1) The seller to whom the information pertains grants consent to disclose the information;

   (2) Disclosure of the information is required by law;

   (3) The information is made public or becomes public by the words or conduct of the seller to whom the information

pertains or from a source other than the seller agent; or

(4) Disclosure is necessary to defend the seller agent against an accusation of wrongful conduct in a judicial proceeding before the commission or before a professional committee; and

G. Must be able to promote alternative properties not owned by the seller to prospective buyers as well as list competing properties for sale without breaching any duty to the client.

2. **Duty to buyer.** The duty of a seller agent to a buyer is governed by the following.

A. A seller agent shall treat all prospective buyers honestly and may not knowingly give false information and shall disclose in a timely manner to a prospective buyer all material defects pertaining to the physical condition of the property of which the seller agent knew or, acting in a reasonable manner, should have known. A seller agent is not liable to a buyer for providing false information to the buyer if the false information was provided to the seller agent by the seller agent's client and the seller agent did not know or, acting in a reasonable manner, should not have known that the information was false. A seller agent is not obligated to discover latent defects in the property.

B. Nothing in this subchapter precludes the obligation of a buyer to inspect the physical condition of the property. A cause of action may not arise on behalf of any person against a seller agent for revealing information in compliance with this subchapter.

C. A seller agent may provide assistance to the buyer by performing ministerial acts such as preparing offers and conveying those offers to the seller and providing information and assistance concerning professional services not related to real estate brokerage services. Performing ministerial acts for the buyer may not be construed as violating the seller agent's agreement with the seller or forming a brokerage agreement with the buyer. Performing ministerial acts for the buyer does not make the seller agent a transaction broker for the buyer.

§13274. BUYER AGENT

1 **Duty to buyer.** A buyer agent:

A. Shall perform the terms of the brokerage agreement made with the buyer;

B. Shall promote the interests of the buyer by exercising agency duties as set forth in section 13272 including:

    (1) Seeking a property at a price and terms specified by the buyer except that the buyer agent is not obligated to seek other properties for the buyer while the buyer is a party to a contract to purchase that property unless it is provided by the brokerage agreement;

    (2) Presenting in a timely manner all offers to and from the buyer;

    (3) Disclosing to the buyer material facts of which the buyer agent has actual knowledge or, if acting in a reasonable manner, should have known concerning the transaction, except as directed in section 13280. Nothing in this subchapter limits any obligation of a buyer to inspect the physical condition of the property;

    (4) Advising the buyer to obtain expert advice on material matters that are beyond the expertise of the buyer agent; and

    (5) Accounting in a timely manner for all money and property received in which the buyer has or may have an interest;

C. Shall exercise reasonable skill and care, except that a buyer agent is not obligated to discover latent defects in the property;

D. Shall comply with all requirements of the laws governing real estate commission brokerage licenses and any rules adopted by the commission;

E. Shall comply with any applicable federal, state or local laws, rules, regulations or ordinances related to real estate brokerage including fair housing and civil rights laws or regulations;

F. Has an obligation to preserve confidential information provided by the buyer during the course of the relationship that might have a negative impact on the buyer's real estate activity unless:

    (1) The buyer to whom the information pertains grants consent to disclose the information;

    (2) Disclosure of the information is required by law;

    (3) The information is made public or becomes public by the words or conduct of the buyer to whom the information pertains or from a source other than the buyer agent; or

    (4) Disclosure is necessary to defend the buyer agent against an action of wrongful conduct in a judicial proceeding before the commission or before a professional committee; and

G. Must be able to promote other properties in which the buyer is interested to other buyers who might also be clients of the buyer agent without breaching any duty or obligation.

2. Duty to seller. The duty of a buyer agent to a seller is governed by the following.

A. A buyer agent shall treat all prospective sellers honestly and may not knowingly give them false information including material facts about the buyer's financial ability to perform the terms of the transaction.

B. A buyer agent is not liable to a seller for providing false information to the seller if the false information was provided to the buyer agent by the buyer agent's client and the buyer agent did not know or, acting in a reasonable manner, should not have known that the information was false. A cause of action may not arise on behalf of any person against a buyer agent for revealing information in compliance with this subchapter.

C. A buyer agent may provide assistance to the seller by performing ministerial acts such as preparing and conveying offers to the buyer and providing information and assistance concerning professional services not related to real estate brokerage services. Performing ministerial acts for the seller may not be construed as violating the buyer agent's agreement with the buyer or forming a brokerage agreement with the seller. Performing ministerial acts for the seller does not make the buyer agent a transaction broker for the seller.

§13275. DISCLOSED DUAL AGENT

1. Consent agreement; disclosed dual agent. A real estate brokerage agency may act as a disclosed dual agent only with the informed written consent of all parties. Consent is presumed to be informed if the party signs an agreement that contains the following:

A. A description of the transactions in which the real estate brokerage agency will serve as a disclosed dual agent;

B. A statement that, in serving as a disclosed dual agent, the real estate brokerage agency represents 2 clients whose interests are adverse and that the agency duties are limited;

C. A statement that the disclosed dual agent may disclose any information to one party that the disclosed dual agent gains from the other party if that information is relevant to the transaction, except:

(1) The willingness or ability of the seller to accept less than the asking price;

(2) The willingness or ability of the buyer to pay more than has been offered;

(3) Confidential negotiating strategy not disclosed in the sales offer as terms of the sale; and

(4) The motivation of the seller for selling and the motivation of the buyer for buying;

D. A statement that the client may choose to consent or not consent to the disclosed dual agency; and

E. A statement that the consent of the client has been given voluntarily and that the agreement has been read and understood.

2. **Cause of action.** A cause of action may not be brought on behalf of any person against a disclosed dual agent for making disclosures permitted or required by this subchapter and the disclosed dual agent does not terminate any client relationship by making disclosures permitted or required by this subchapter.

3. **Actual knowledge; information.** In a disclosed dual agent situation each client and the real estate brokerage agency and its affiliated licensees are considered to possess only actual knowledge and information. There is no imputation of knowledge or information by operation of law among or between the clients, the real estate brokerage agency or its affiliated licensees.

4. **Duty to parties.** The duty of a disclosed dual agent to the client who is selling is the same as set forth in section 13273, and the duty to the client who is buying is the same as set forth in section 13274, except that:

A. A disclosed dual agent may not promote the interests of one party to the detriment of the other party except as required to comply with this section; and

B. A disclosed dual agent may disclose any information to one party that the disclosed dual agent gains from the other party if that information is relevant to the transaction, except:

(1) The willingness or ability of the seller to accept less than the asking price;

(2) The willingness or ability of the buyer to pay more than has been offered;

(3) Confidential negotiating strategy not disclosed in the sales offer as terms of the sale; and

(4) The motivation of the seller for selling and the motivation of the buyer for buying.

§13276. INTERPRETATION

The provisions of this subchapter supersede the duties and responsibilities of the parties under the common law, including fiduciary responsibilities of an agent to a client or principal, except with regard to vicarious liability and except as set forth in this subchapter. This section does not preclude the use of common law, when it is not inconsistent with this subchapter, in defining and interpreting the duties listed in section 13272. This section does not abrogate an injured party's cause of action pursuant to this chapter.

§13277. WRITTEN POLICY

Every real estate brokerage agency shall adopt a written company policy that identifies and describes the types of real estate brokerage relationships in which the designated broker and affiliated licensees may engage.

§13278. APPOINTED AGENTS WITHIN A FIRM

1. **Appointed agents.** A real estate brokerage agency entering into a brokerage agreement may, through the designated broker, appoint in writing to the client those affiliated licensees within the real estate brokerage agency who will be acting as appointed agents of that client to the exclusion of all other affiliated licensees within the real estate brokerage agency.

2. **Not a dual agent.** A real estate brokerage agency and the designated broker are not considered to be dual agents solely because of an appointment under the provisions of this section, except that any affiliated licensee who personally represents both the seller and the buyer, as clients, in a particular transaction is considered to be a dual agent and is required to comply with the provisions of this subchapter governing disclosed dual agents.

3. **Actual knowledge; information.** When agents are appointed, each client, the real estate brokerage agency and its appointed licensees are considered to possess only actual knowledge and information. There is no imputation of knowledge or information by operation of law among or between the clients, the real estate brokerage agency and appointed agents.

4. **Appointments; roles.** Methods of appointment and the role of the real

estate brokerage agency and the designated broker must be defined by rules adopted by the commission. The rules must include a requirement that clients be informed as to the real estate brokerage agency's appointed agent policy and give written consent to that policy in advance of entering into a brokerage agreement.

§13279. REAL ESTATE BROKERAGE RELATIONSHIP DISCLOSURE REQUIRED

A real estate brokerage agency shall provide in a timely manner to buyers and sellers of residential real property a meaningful, written real estate brokerage relationship disclosure form as defined and mandated by rules adopted by the commission. For purposes of this section, "residential real property" means real estate consisting of not less than one nor more than 4 residential dwelling units.

§13280. REAL ESTATE COMMISSION RULES

The commission shall adopt rules setting forth criteria necessary to the implementation of this subchapter.The rules must include, but are not limited to, the following:

1. **Disclosure.** Those aspects of the services of a real estate brokerage agency and its affiliated licensees that must be disclosed to a client; and

2. **Handling of information.** Procedures to be followed by a real estate brokerage agency and its affiliated licensees to prevent the mishandling of information and undisclosed dual agency in the representation of clients. In adopting these rules, the commission shall consider the formal and informal sharing of information within a real estate brokerage agency, the arrangement of real estate brokerage agency office space, the relationships of affiliated licensees within a real estate brokerage agency who are representing clients with adverse interests and means of avoiding client representation by an undisclosed dual agent. The commission shall review the professional responsibility rules and practices of the legal profession with regard to conflict of interest in considering the adoption of rules under this subsection.

§13281. DURATION OF THE RELATIONSHIP

1. **Effective date.** The relationships set forth in this subchapter commence on the effective date of the real estate brokerage agency's

brokerage agreement and continue until performance, completion, termination or expiration of that brokerage agreement.

2. **Obligation; termination.** A real estate brokerage agency and an affiliated licensee owe no further duty or obligation after termination, expiration, completion or performance of the brokerage agreement, except the duties of:

A. Accounting in a timely manner for all money and property related to, and received during, the relationship; and

B. For seller agents, buyer agents, subagents and disclosed dual agents, treating as confidential information provided by the client during the course of the relationship that could have a negative impact on the client's real estate activity, unless:

(1) The client to whom the information pertains grants written consent;

(2) Disclosure of the information is required by law;

(3) The information is made public or becomes public by the words or conduct of the client to whom the information pertains or from a source other than the real estate brokerage agency or the affiliated licensee; or

(4) Disclosure is necessary to defend the real estate brokerage agency or an affiliated licensee against an action of wrongful conduct in a judicial proceeding before the commission or before a professional committee.

§13282. PRESUMPTION

Except as otherwise provided in this subchapter, a real estate brokerage agency providing real estate brokerage services is presumed to be acting as a transaction broker unless the real estate brokerage agency has agreed, in a written brokerage agreement, to represent one or more parties to the real estate transaction as the real estate brokerage agency's clients. Client representation may not be created orally or by implication or be assumed by a real estate brokerage agency or any party to a real estate transaction

§13283. TRANSACTION BROKER

1. **Not an agent.** A transaction broker does not represent any party as a client to a real estate transaction and is not bound by the duties set forth in section 13272.

2. **Responsibilities.** A transaction broker shall:

A. Account in a timely manner for all money and property received;

B. Disclose in a timely manner to a buyer to a transaction all material defects pertaining to the physical condition of the property of which the transaction broker has actual notice or knowledge;

C. Comply with all requirements of the laws governing real estate commission brokerage licenses and any rules adopted by the commission;

D. Comply with any applicable federal, state or local laws, rules, regulations or ordinances related to real estate brokerage, including fair housing and civil rights laws or regulations;

E. Treat all parties honestly and may not knowingly give false information; and

F. Perform such ministerial acts as may be agreed upon between the transaction broker and one or more parties to a real estate transaction.

A transaction broker is not liable for providing false information if the false information was provided to the transaction broker and the transaction broker did not know that the information was false. A transaction broker is not obligated to discover latent defects in the property. A cause of action does not arise on behalf of any person against a transaction broker who reveals information or makes disclosures permitted or required by this subchapter.

3. Prohibited acts. A transaction broker may not:

A. Conduct an inspection, investigation or analysis of a property for the benefit of any party;

B. Verify the accuracy or completeness of oral or written statements made by the seller or buyer or any 3rd party; or

C. Promote the interests of either party to a transaction except as required to comply with this section.

4. No vicarious liability. A party to a real estate transaction is not vicariously liable for the acts or omissions of a transaction broker.

5. Actual knowledge; information. In a situation in which one affiliated licensee acting as an appointed agent of a real estate brokerage agency represents a party to a real estate transaction as the real estate brokerage agency's client and another affiliated licensee of the same real estate brokerage agency is acting as a transaction broker for another party to the transaction, the real estate brokerage agency and its affiliated licensees are considered to possess only actual knowledge and information. There is no imputation of knowledge or information by operation of law among or between the parties, the real estate brokerage agency or its affiliated licensees.

RULES OF MAINE REAL ESTATE COMMISSION

Chapter 300: GENERAL INFORMATION

SUMMARY: This rule establishes guidelines relating to meetings, agendas, maintenance of records and filing of documents or fees.

Section 1. Meetings

Meetings shall be called by the Chairman or a majority of the members whenever such meetings are deemed necessary for carrying out the business of the Commission, but the Commission shall not meet less than four times a year.

Section 2. Meeting Notices

The Director shall be responsible for distributing meeting notices to the members and to others as required by statute or rule. Notices may also be provided to others deemed to have an interest in the business before the Commission.

Section 3. Meeting Agendas

A. An agenda for meetings shall be prepared by the Director and shall include business requiring consideration or action by the members. The agenda shall also include all business items requested by the members provided such request is received by the Director at least seven (7) days in advance of the meeting.

B. Business not included on the agenda may be considered following an affirmative vote of a majority of the members present.

Section 4. Records

The Director shall have custody of the Commission seal and shall maintain a record of all business conducted by the Commission. The Director shall preserve, subject to the provisions of 5 M.R.S.A. Chapter 6, all books, documents and papers entrusted to his care. Records shall be opened to public inspection subject to 1 M.R.S.A. Chapter 13. Delays in making records available for inspection may be occasioned by action necessary to preserve the security of records, to obtain legal advice, or to avoid disrupting regular business activities and for these reasons it is recommended that requests be submitted three (3) business days in advance of anticipated inspection.

Access to written communication with the Assistant Attorney General, criminal history records, materials relating to license examinations and other records may be restricted subject to 1 M.R.S.A. Chapter 13.

Section 5. Filing of Applications, Documents and Fees

Whenever the statutes or rules specify filing with the Commission it shall be construed to mean the Director of the Commission. The Director shall be responsible for transmitting the information to the members if notice or action by the members is required. Timely filing with the Director shall be considered timely filing with the members.

Section 6. Chairman

The Chairman shall be elected by the members at the first meeting in December of each year and shall take office on the following January 1st. The Commission members may also elect a Vice Chairman to preside over meetings in the absence of the Chairman.

CHAPTER 310 ADVISORY RULINGS

SUMMARY: This chapter details procedures for submission, consideration, and disposition of requests for advisory rulings.

Section 1. Authority and Scope

The Commission may issue an advisory ruling pursuant to 5 M.R.S.A. §9001 concerning the applicability to an existing factual situation of any statutes or rules it administers. Each request shall be reviewed individually by the Director to determine whether an advisory ruling is appropriate. The Director may decline the request for an advisory ruling when the question is hypothetical, if there is insufficient experience upon which to base a ruling, or for any other reason deemed proper. The denial of a request may be appealed to the Commission by providing written notice to the Director within twenty (20) days following the denial.

Section 2. Submission

A request for an advisory ruling shall be submitted to the Director in writing and shall set forth in detail all facts pertinent to the question. The Director may require additional information as necessary to complete a factual background for a ruling of the Commission.

Section 3. Acknowledgment

A request for an advisory ruling shall be acknowledged by the Director within ten (10) days of receipt. Within thirty (30) days the Director shall provide notification that a request for ruling shall or shall not be presented to the Commission, or the Director may request additional information which is necessary to determine whether or not an advisory ruling is appropriate.

An advisory ruling shall be in writing and shall include a statement of facts or assumptions, or both, upon which the ruling is based. The statement, without reference to other documents, shall be sufficiently detailed to allow understanding of the basis of the opinion. A ruling shall be rendered with the assent of four (4) members of the Commission. An advisory ruling shall be signed by the Chairman of the Commission, shall be identified specifically as an advisory ruling, and shall be numbered serially.

Section 4. Disposition

An advisory ruling shall be mailed to the requesting party and a copy shall be kept by the Director. An advisory ruling is a public document and shall be available for public inspection during normal working hours of the Commission. In addition, the Commission, as it deems appropriate, may otherwise publish or circulate an advisory ruling.

CHAPTER 340 COMPLAINTS AND INVESTIGATIONS

SUMMARY: This rule establishes guidelines and procedures for filing complaints, conducting investigations and disposition of matters following investigations.

Section 1. Verified Complaints

A copy of a written verified complaint, signed under oath, alleging activities in violation of 32 M.R.S.A. Chapter114 or concerning the qualifications of any Commission licensee, shall be sent by regular mail to the last known address of the person against whom the complaint is filed and his designated broker together with a request for a written response to the allegation. The investigation may also include such other inquiries as may be deemed appropriate in order to complete the processing of the complaint according to the provisions of 32 M.R.S.A. §13067 or §13174.

Section 2. Other Investigations

An investigation may be conducted based upon information other than a verified complaint if such information provides prima facie evidence of a violation of 32 M.R.S.A. Chapter 114, or if the information raises a substantial question regarding the qualifications of any applicant or licensee.

Section 3. Member Request for Investigation

A member of the Commission may file a complaint or request an investigation, but such complaint or request shall serve to disqualify the member from participating in a hearing or a consent agreement regarding the issue. He shall be prohibited from discussing the issue with other members, except as a witness or party, until after final agency action and the time for appeal has lapsed or appeal rights have been exhausted.

Section 4. Prohibited Communications

The members shall avoid discussing, except with adequate notice and opportunity for all parties to participate, any specific case under investigation, or any case which may reasonably be expected to be the subject of investigation, until after final agency action and the time for filing an appeal has lapsed or appeal remedies have been exhausted.

This rule shall not be construed to limit the members at Commission meetings from discussion among themselves or with the attorney for the Commission. These rules shall not be construed to limit communications regarding closed matters, investigations in general, inquiries regarding the status of a specific case, or other matters not relating to issues of fact or law concerning a specific case.

Chapter 350: ADJUDICATORY HEARINGS

SUMMARY: This rule establishes policies, guidelines and procedures relating to adjudicatory proceedings which come before the Commission.

Section 1. Hearings in General

Commission hearings shall conform to the Administrative Procedures Act 5 M.R.S.A. Chapter 375.

Section 2. Duties and Responsibilities of the Chairman

The Chairman or an alternate designated by the Commission shall preside at a hearing in a manner affording consideration of fair play and compliance with the constitutional requirements of due process. The Chairman shall also have authority to:
  A. Hold a conference for the simplification of issues;
  B. Issue subpoenas requested by the parties;
  C. Place witnesses under oath;
  D. Take action necessary to maintain order;
  E. Rule on motions and procedural questions arising during the hearing;
  F. Call recesses or adjourn the hearing; and
  G. Prescribe and enforce general rules of conduct and decorum.

Section 3. Role of Commission Members

The members collectively shall be responsible for reviewing evidence and hearing testimony and argument in order to:
  A. Determine whether or not the alleged conduct was supported by the evidence;
  B. Determine whether or not the conduct was a violation of 32 M.R.S.A. Chapter 114 and/or related rules;
  C. Determine and impose appropriate sanctions; and
  D. Determine whether or not to issue cease and desist orders, and to issue such orders.

Section 4. Ex Parte Communications

A member shall not discuss an issue of fact or law concerning a case or pending appeal which comes before the Commission, except with notice and opportunity for participation by all parties. This rule shall not be construed to limit a discussion that does not relate to the merits of a case, such as scheduling or procedural issues. A member shall not be limited from discussing a case at meetings with the attorney for the Commission.

Section 5. Parties

Parties in a Commission hearing, with the exception of the Director or the Director's designee and anintervener, shall be limited to:
  A. The person against whom the allegation is made; or
  B. The person whose qualifications are in question.

Section 6. Intervention

An application for intervention in a Commission proceeding shall be filed, except for good cause shown, at least seven (7) days in advance of the scheduled hearing. Rulings by the Chairman shall be subject to the provisions of 5 M.R.S.A. §9054.

Section 7. Order of Proceedings

The order of proceedings, unless modified by the Chairman to facilitate the hearing, shall be as follows:

    A. The party bringing the action may offer an opening statement;

    B. The party defending against the action may offer an opening statement;

    C. The party presenting evidence in support of the action may offer his case;

    D. The party defending against the action may cross examine each witness;

    E. The party defending against the action may offer his case;

    F. The party in support of the action may cross examine each witness; and

    G. Each party may offer a closing statement at the hearing or in writing within seven (7) business days following the hearing.

Section 8. Subpoenas

A party shall be entitled to the issuance of subpoenas in the name of the Commission subject to the provisions of 5 M.R.S.A. §9060. Subpoenas shall be requested, except for good cause, at least ten (10) days in advance of a scheduled hearing. Subpoenaed witnesses shall be paid the same fees for attendance and travel as in civil cases before the courts. Fees shall be paid by the party requesting the subpoenas when the request is submitted.

Section 9. Appeals of Director's Decisions

The decision of the Director may be appealed in any of the following circumstances:

    A. Denial of an examination for licensing; or,

    B. Denial of a license or license renewal.

The appeal for a hearing before the Commission shall be in writing within thirty (30) days following thereceipt of the decision of the Director.

Section 10. Notice of Hearings

Notice of a hearing shall be given to all parties at least ten (10) days prior to the date on which the hearing is to be held.

Chapter 360: PREREQUISITES TO LICENSURE BY INDIVIDU-ALS

Summary: This chapter establishes the educational guidelines which must be met by individuals in order to qualify for licensure under 32 MRSA Chapter 114.

1. Policy Statement

The Commission shall encourage the development and delivery of high quality pre-licensure courses throughout the state. In an effort to heighten professionalism within the real estate industry, the Commission shall encourage degree-granting institutions in the state to develop and deliver such courses.

2. Definitions

1. Qualifying Educational Program

"Qualifying educational program" means a program or course of study which meets one or more of the minimum competencies defined in the Commission-approved models entitled "The Sales Agent Course," "The Associate Broker Course" or "The Designated Broker Course." These courses shall be sponsored by a degree-granting institution, a proprietary school or a public school adult education program that follows the Commission-established procedure for approval.

2. Program Sponsor

A program sponsor shall be defined as that individual, group of individuals, or organization responsible for the development, coordination, administration and delivery of a course or program.

3. Satisfactory Completion

Satisfactory completion of a course or program shall mean having met all minimum requirements established by the sponsor for the course or program and having achieved a grade of at least 75%.

3. Approval of Qualifying Educational Program

1. Syllabus

The program sponsor shall submit the course syllabus, on a form furnished by the director, meeting the minimum course competencies set for each course as described in Section 5 of this chapter for each pre-licensure course offered. The syllabus, at a minimum, must contain:

    A. Name, address, phone number of the sponsor;
    B. Name, address, phone number of the instructor;
    C. Course title;
    D. Course start and end dates;
    E. Class session times;
    F. Course text titles and publishers;
    G. A class session-by-session breakdown of the content and con-cepts to be covered, with quiz and test dates noted;
    H. Grading policy;
    I. Attendance policy; and
    J. Final course examination and answer key.

The course sponsor shall submit the syllabus and the filing fee to the director at least 30 days prior to the first class session. A syllabus received less than 30 days prior to the first class session will be as-sessed a late filing fee.

2. Reporting Program Changes

The course sponsor shall report any substantial change in a submitted or approved course syllabus to the director.

3. Syllabus Review

The director, within 30 days of receipt of a complete syllabus, shall notify the sponsor, in writing, of the
approval or denial of the syllabus.

4. Appeal of Denial to the Director

A sponsor who is aggrieved by denial of syllabus approval may re-quest a hearing to appeal the decision. Such request shall be made in writing, and shall be submitted within 30 days of receipt of the denial of the syllabus.

5. Distribution of Course Guidelines and Syllabus

At the first class session, the sponsor shall disseminate to students the course guidelines developed by the Commission and the syllabus.

6. Advance Notice to Course Participants

Upon commencement of the first class session of a pre-licensure course, the instructor shall read and distribute to the students one of the following statements. If the syllabus for the course has been approved, Statement #1 is to be read. If the syllabus for the course has not been submitted or the course has not received approval, Statement #2 is to be read.

Statement #1 – "The Maine Real Estate Commission is committed to quality real estate education. Toward this goal, the syllabus for this pre-license course has been reviewed and approved as meeting the guidelines established by the Commission. These guidelines and the syllabus have been distributed for your information. At the end of this course, you will be given an opportunity to critique this course and its delivery. The Commission welcomes your comments regarding your experience in this course."

Statement #2 – "The Maine Real Estate Commission is committed to quality real estate education. To achieve this goal, the syllabus for each pre-license course must be submitted and approved before the course is promoted as meeting pre-license requirements. The syllabus for this course has not been approved. Unless and until it is approved, you may not assume that successful completion of this course will qualify you for licensure".

---

7. Student Enrollment Report

The course sponsor shall be responsible for submitting a completed enrollment report, in a format approved by the director, within 30 days of the completion of each pre-license course.

8. Evaluations Required

The course sponsor shall distribute course evaluation forms to students for their critique of the learning experience. A summary of the student evaluations shall be submitted to the director with the enrollment report.

9. Transcripts

The course sponsor shall provide a course transcript to students successfully completing the course. Such transcript shall, at a minimum, include the course title, student's name, final numerical grade, beginning and course completion date and be signed by the course sponsor.

10. Disciplinary Action

Approval of pre-license courses may be revoked or suspended for violation of this chapter.

11. Prohibition Against Recruiting

The course sponsor shall not allow anyone to use the school's premises or classroom to recruit new affiliates for any real estate brokerage company.

4. Educational Requirements For Licensure

1. Real Estate Broker

An applicant who has been licensed as an associate broker affiliated with a real estate brokerage agency for 2 years within the 5 years immediately preceding the date of application must submit evidence of satisfactory completion of a qualifying educational program which covers the minimum competencies defined in the Commission-approved model entitled "The Designated Broker Course." The application for licensure must be submitted within one year of completion of this educational program.

2. Associate Real Estate Broker

An applicant who has practiced as a real estate sales agent for 2 years within the 5 years immediately preceding the date of application must submit a course transcript confirming that the applicant successfully completed the qualifying educational program which covers the minimum competencies defined in the Commission-approved model entitled "The Associate Broker Course."

3. Real Estate Sales Agent

As a prerequisite to examination, an applicant for a sales agent license must, within one year of completion of the course, submit a course transcript confirming that the applicant successfully completed a qualifying educational program which covers the minimum competencies defined in the Commission-approved model entitled "The Sales Agent Course".

5. Commission Established Minimum Competencies

1. Generally

The Commission shall establish minimum competency requirements for all levels and types of licensure. Educational models and examinations shall be designed to satisfy these requirements.

2. Annual Review

The Commission, on an annual basis, shall review the minimum competencies required for all levels and types of licensure.

Chapter 370: CONTINUING EDUCATION

SUMMARY: This rule sets forth the policy and guidelines for review and approval of programs which will be accepted for credit toward continuing education requirements for license renewal.

Section 1. Policy Statement

The Commission shall encourage the development and delivery of high quality real estate educational programs, and, in an effort to stimulate opportunity for professional growth of licensees, shall encourage development and delivery of programs at graduated levels of study.

In reviewing and approving a program application, the Director shall consider:

A. Program content as it contributes to the ability of the licensee to serve and meet the needs of his clients and customers;

B. Program content as it assists a licensee to keep informed concerning real estate laws, regulations, and practices;

C. Geographic availability to licensees.

Section 2. Definition of Terms

A. <u>Real Estate Educational Program.</u> Real estate educational program shall be defined as a planned learning experience of at least two (2) hours, designed to promote development of knowledge, skills, and attitudes pertaining to real estate brokerage.

B. <u>Program Sponsor.</u> A Program Sponsor shall be defined as that individual, group of individuals, or organization responsible for the development, coordination, administration and delivery of a program.

C. <u>Program Instructor.</u> A Program Instructor shall be defined as an individual appointed to impart knowledge or information to licensees participating in a program.

D. <u>Distance Education.</u> A continuing education distance education course is a program whereby instruction does not take place in a traditional classroom setting but rather where teacher and student are apart and instruction takes place through other media. Distance education programs include but are not limited to those which are presented through interactive classrooms, computer conferencing, interactive computer, the internet and by written correspondence course.

E. Core Educational Requirement. A core educational requirement shall be defined as a three hour course which includes all of the Commission approved components for a core course. The commission prescribed curriculum for this course may be obtained from the Director.

Section 3. Program Criteria

A. Subject Matter. Consistent with 32 M.R.S.A. §13197, the following real estate related topics shall be acceptable subject matter for educational programs:
1. Property valuation;
2. Construction;
3. Contract and agency law;
4. Financing and investments;
5. Land use, planning, zoning and other public limitations on ownership;
6. Landlord-tenant relationships;
7. License laws, rules and standards of professional practice;
8. Taxation;
9. Timeshares, condominiums and cooperatives;
10. Staff supervision and training;
11. Office management;
12. Any additional topic which is approved by the Director.

B. Examination. Each distance education course must include a comprehensive examination to be completed by the licensee before a grade or credit may be awarded. A copy of the examination must accompany the application for program approval.

Section 4. Administrative Procedure

A. Applications. An application adopted by the Commission for program approval shall be furnished by the Director. This application shall require information on the following:
1. Sponsor;
2. Instructor qualifications;
3. Content and methodology;
4. Length of program;
5. Learning objectives;
6. Assessment of learning objectives;
7. Requirement for completion.

The completed application and the fee shall be submitted to the Director. Applications submitted after the first
course session will be assessed a late filing fee.

B. Program Evaluation. A program evaluation shall be required and the results shall be made available to the Director upon request. An evaluation form may be obtained from the Director. A summary of student evaluations shall be submitted when an application for renewed approval is submitted.

C. Reporting Program Changes. A change in a submitted or approved program application shall be reported to the Director. A change in program content or instructor shall be reviewed and approved in advance of the scheduled program.

D. Program Approval. The Director, within thirty (30) days of receipt of a completed application, shall notify the sponsor, in writing, of the terms and duration of the approval, or the reasons for denial.

E. Appeal of the Decision of the Director to "Deny Program Approval." A sponsor who is aggrieved by denial of program approval may request a hearing to appeal the decision. Such request shall be made in writing, and shall be submitted within thirty (30) days of receipt of denial of application.

F. Program Completion. The sponsor, following program delivery, shall issue a certificate of course completion to each licensee successfully completing the course and prepare a roster of licensees successfully completing the course. The sponsor shall retain the roster of licensees completing the course for a period of not less than three (3) years.

G. Program Renewal. An application adopted by the commission for program renewal shall be furnished by the Director. This application shall require information on the following:

    1. Sponsor;
    2. Instructor;
    3. Length of program;
    4. Title;
    5. Program approval number;
    6. List of dates, times, and locations course was held;
    7. List of future dates, times, and locations;
    8. Statement by sponsor on the extent to which the identified learning objectives were met;

9. Description of any changes implemented to ensure that the learning objectives will be met in the future; and
10. Summary of student evaluations

H. Approval Expiration. Sponsors who promote and conduct continuing education courses as approved once the course approval has expired, may be subject to suspension or revocation of approval of additional continuing education courses.

Section 5. Program Advertisement

An advertisement for an educational program shall include the following:

A. A course description sufficient to identify the subject matter to be covered;
B. Identification of the level of instruction;
C. Identification of the method or format of instruction;
D. A statement of program objectives; and
E. Notice indicating the program has been approved by the Director for continuing education and the number of clock hours to be received upon satisfactory completion of the program.

Section 6. Advance Notice to Program Participants

Upon commencement of each program, participants shall be informed of the following:

"This program has been approved by the Director of the Real Estate Commission for clock hours toward fulfillment of the educational requirements for renewal of a real estate license.

"The Commission is interested in the quality and delivery of educational programs which are offered to licensees and, therefore, welcomes and encourages comments regarding program subject matter and quality of the delivery of the program."

Section 7. Limitations on Obtaining Clock Hours

A. A licensee shall complete an educational program in its entirety in order to be eligible for continuing education approval.
B. A licensee, for purposes of renewal or reactivation, shall use only those clock hours which were accumulated during the two (2) years immediately preceding such renewal or activation.
C. An instructor who teaches an approved program shall receive clock hour approval for that program only once.

D. Licensees who wish to use a continuing education distance education course to activate or renew a real estate license must complete the distance education course with a minimum grade of 85%.

Section 8. Approval of Individual Requests

A. An Educational Program in Which a Sponsor Has Not Submitted An Application for Director Approval. The Director shall consider, on an individual basis, a request by a licensee for approval of a program for which the sponsor did not seek approval, but in which the licensee participated. Approval of such a request shall be subject to the program meeting the standards and criteria required by the Director for other educational programs. The licensee shall be responsible for submitting to the Director a completed program application and fee.

B. Research and Real Estate Related Projects. A licensee may obtain continuing education clock hours, for real estate related research from which a report, article, or thesis results, or for participation in real estate related projects, provided that the director finds that the effort has enhanced the ability of the licensee to meet the needs of his clients and customers. The licensee shall be responsible for submitting documentation and the fee for individual review to the Director.

Section 9. Disciplinary Action

Approval of continuing educational programs may be revoked or suspended for violation of this chapter

Section 10. Core Educational Requirement

A. As of January 1, 1994, no real estate license may be renewed or activated unless the licensee has completed a three hour continuing education program approved as meeting the core educational requirement.

B. The Commission, on an annual basis, shall review the prescribed curriculum for the core educational requirement.

Chapter 400: AGENCY/DESIGNATED BROKER RESPONSIBILI-TIES

Summary: This chapter details requirements of maintaining a real estate brokerage agency and establishes the specific supervisory responsibilities of the designated broker.

1. Responsibilities of Designated Broker

1. Generally

The designated broker shall supervise the activities of affiliated licensees, the activities of unlicensed persons affiliated with the real estate brokerage agency and the operation of the real estate brokerage agency. The supervision includes, at a minimum, the establishment of policies and procedures that enable the designated broker to review, manage and oversee the following:

    A. The real estate transactions performed by an affiliated licensee;

    B. Documents that may have a material effect upon the rights or obligations of a party to a real estate transaction;

    C. The filing, storage and maintenance of such documents;

    D. The handling of money received by the real estate brokerage agency for the parties to a real estate transaction;

    E. The advertising of any service for which a real estate license is required;

    F. The familiarization by the affiliated licensee with the requirements of federal and state law governing real estate transactions

    G. The dissemination, in a timely manner, to affiliated licensees of all regulatory information received by the real estate brokerage agency pertaining to the practice of real estate brokerage.

    H. The registration of any domain name for a web site in order to promote real estate brokerage services or the sale or purchase of real estate through the agency; and

    I. The development or uploading to the internet of a web site that promotes real estate brokerage services or the sale or purchase of real estate through the agency.

2. Monitoring Compliance

The designated broker shall establish a system for monitoring compliance with such policies, rules, procedures and systems, that includes regular meetings with affiliated licensees, company policy manuals, training programs and materials and availability of designated broker to assist and advise.

3. Delegation

The designated broker may designate another person to assist in administering the provisions of the Commission's rules. However, the designated broker does not relinquish overall responsibility for the supervision of affiliated licensees and unlicensed persons affiliated with the real estate brokerage agency.

4. Company Policy

The designated broker shall have a written company policy that identifies and describes the types of real estate brokerage relationships in which the real estate brokerage agency may engage. In addition, the company policy must also include the procedures intended to prevent any mishandling of information through both formal and informal sharing of information within the real estate brokerage agency, the arrangement of agency office space and the personal relationships of affiliated licensees who are representing buyers and sellers with adverse interests.

5. Review of Sales Agent Documents

The designated broker, at a minimum, shall review and initial, as soon as possible, all contracts, property data sheets, disclosure forms, market analyses and other relevant information prepared by a sales agent for buyers and sellers during the first 90 days of the licensing of the sales agent with the real estate brokerage agency. The requirements of this Section are not intended to affect the validity of a contract.

2. Real Estate Trust Accounts

1. Definition of "Earnest Money Deposit"

As used in this Section, the term "earnest money deposit" includes earnest money deposits and all other money held by the real estate brokerage agency for clients or other persons for purposes related to a real estate brokerage transaction.

2. Various Forms of Real Estate Trust Accounts

A real estate trust account shall be in the form of a checking or savings account and may accrue interest on an earnest money deposit provided that the accumulated interest is properly disbursed. If the parties to the transaction agree to place the earnest money deposit in something other than a real estate trust account, the real estate brokerage agency shall not hold the funds or act as trustee.

3. Opening a Real Estate Trust Account

The real estate trust account checks and bank statements must contain the real estate brokerage agency's trade name as licensed by the commission and must be imprinted with the words "real estate trust account."

4. Making Earnest Money Deposits

An earnest money deposit received by a designated broker, as trustee, shall be deposited within 5 business days of acceptance of the offer. Other earnest money deposits received by the trustee shall be deposited within 5 business days of the trustee's receipt of such earnest money deposits.

5. Restrictions on Earnest Money Deposits in Real Estate Trust Accounts

A designated broker shall not commingle the earnest money deposit of buyers or sellers in a real estate transaction with:

A. Funds belonging to the real estate brokerage agency. This provision shall not be construed to limit deposits made by the real estate brokerage agency of an amount sufficient to maintain the account, but such amount shall not exceed $500; or

B. Funds held for persons that do not involve the sale, purchase or exchange of real estate.

An earnest money deposit shall not be utilized prior to a closing for selling or buying expenses such as a title fee, survey, etc., unless agreed to in writing by all parties in the transaction. There shall be a proper accounting for all monies held by the real estate brokerage agency and any remittance shall be made within a reasonable time, but not more than 30 days, after the conclusion of the transaction. An earnest money deposit shall not be utilized prior to a closing for selling or buying expenses such as a title fee, survey, etc., unless agreed to in writing by all parties in the transaction. There shall be a proper accounting for all monies held by the real estate brokerage agency and any remittance shall be made within a reasonable time, but not more than 30 days, after the conclusion of the transaction.

6. Maintaining Real Estate Trust Account Records

The designated broker shall maintain records and supporting documents sufficient to verify the adequacy and proper use of the real estate trust account. The records and supporting documents shall be maintained for a period of at least 3 years after the date set forth in Section 7(G) of this chapter.

7. Information Included in Minimum Real Estate Trust Account Records

Minimum real estate trust account records shall include a ledger or journal which records in chronological order all receipts and disbursements of funds in the real estate trust account and provides the following information:

- A. The date the earnest money deposit is received by the real estate brokerage agency;
- B. The date the earnest money deposit is received by the banking institution;
- C. The purpose of the earnest money deposit and from whom received;
- D. The purpose of the withdrawal and to whom paid;
- E. The amount of the earnest money deposit;
- F. The current running balance of funds held by the real estate brokerage agency; and
- G. The closing date of a transaction, if any, or the date the earnest money deposit was disbursed.

8. Real Estate Trust Account Supporting Documents

Real estate trust account supporting documents shall include:

- A. Bank statements;
- B. Canceled checks;
- C. Copies of contracts;
- D. Closing statements, if available;
- E. Correspondence; and
- F. Additional items necessary to verify and explain record entries.

9. Disbursement of Undisputed Earnest Money Deposits Held in Trust

Disbursement of an undisputed earnest money deposit may occur by one of the two following procedures:

- A. Authorization, in writing, from the parties to a real estate brokerage transaction agreeing to the disbursement; or
- B. Authorization by the designated broker who, in reasonable reliance on the terms of the purchase and sale agreement or other written documents signed by both parties, determines

the appropriate disbursement of the undisputed earnest money deposit. The designated broker may, at the designated broker's own discretion, make such disbursement to release the undisputed earnest money deposit no sooner than 5 business days after notifying both parties of the designated broker's proposed decision to release the undisputed earnest money deposit. The earnest money deposit shall not be disbursed under this Section if prior to disbursement the designated broker receives actual knowledge of a dispute as provided in Section 2(10) of this chapter.

10. Disputed Earnest Money

    A. Any time that more than one party to a transaction makes demand on the earnest money deposit for which the real estate brokerage agency is acting as trustee, the designated broker shall:

        (1) Notify each party, in writing, of the demand of the other party; and

        (2) Keep all parties to the transaction informed of any actions by the designated broker regarding the disputed earnest money deposit, including retention of the earnest money deposit by the designated broker until receipt of written release from both parties agreeing to the disposition of the earnest money deposit or agreeing that the dispute has been properly resolved.

    B After notice as provided in Section 2(10)(A)(1) of this chapter, the designated broker may reasonably rely on the terms of the purchase and sale agreement or other written documents signed by both parties to determine the disposition of the disputed earnest money deposit and may, at the designated broker's own discretion, make such disbursement no sooner than 5 business days after notifying both parties of the designated broker's proposed disbursement of the earnest money deposit. This discretionary disbursement by the designated broker is not a violation of license law, but may not relieve the designated broker of civil liability.

    C The designated broker may hold the earnest money deposit until ordered by a court of proper jurisdiction or agreement of the parties to make a disbursement. The designated broker shall give all parties written notice of any decision to hold the earnest money deposit pending a court judgment or agreement of the parties for disbursement.

D. Absent written authorization from the party to be charged, the designated broker is not entitled to withhold any portion of the earnest money deposit when a real estate transaction fails to close even if a commission is earned. The earnest money deposit must be disposed of as provided by Section 2(10) of this chapter.

3. Record Retention Schedules; Format.

1. Generally

All real estate brokerage records, including real estate trust account and supporting records, transaction files, and other brokerage-related records, are to be under the control of the designated broker and made available to the director upon request. Except for rejected offers and counteroffers, which must be kept for one year from the date of the rejected offer or counteroffer, the following records must be kept by the designated broker for 3 calendar years after all funds held by the designated broker in connection with a transaction have been disbursed to the proper party or until the conclusion of the transaction, whichever last occurs:

A. The original or a true copy of all purchase and sale contracts;

B. Listing or buyer brokerage representation agreements, appointed agent consent forms, disclosed dual agent consent forms and the Real Estate Relationships Form required under Chapter 410, Section 9 of the Commission's rules;

C. Property disclosure forms, data sheets and other property information prepared by the real estate brokerage agency or one of its affiliated licensees to promote property for sale or purchase;

D. Real Estate Trust Account ledger records, as listed in Section 2(7) of this chapter; and

E. Real Estate Trust Account reconciliation records, as listed in Section 2(8) of this chapter.

2. Electronic Format

Real estate brokerage records may be maintained in electronic format, as defined by 10 MRSA Chapter 1051. An electronic record means a record generated, communicated, received or stored by electronic means. Such electronic records must be in a format that has the continued capability to be retrieved and legibly printed. Upon request of the director, printed records shall be produced.

4. Examinations for Compliance with Licensing Laws

A real estate brokerage office may be examined for compliance with licensing laws once each licensing period, as necessary as part of an investigation of a complaint filed with the director or may be examined upon receipt of prima facie evidence indicating improper use of a real estate trust account. The designated broker shall produce for inspection by an authorized representative of the Commission any document or record reasonably necessary for investigation or audit in the enforcement of 32 MRSA Chapter 114 and in enforcement of the rules promulgated by the Commission. Failure to submit such documents or records as requested by the director shall be grounds for disciplinary action. The examiner shall notify the agency of the results of such office examination and may file a complaint.

Chapter 410: MINIMUM STANDARDS OF PRACTICE

Summary: This chapter clarifies and establishes standards for practicing real estate brokerage.

1. Advertising

1. Definitions

A. Advertise. "Advertise," "advertising" and "advertisement" include all forms of representation, promotion and solicitation disseminated in any manner and by any means of communication for any purpose related to real estate brokerage activity, including, at a minimum, advertising the sale or purchase of real estate or promotion of real estate brokerage services conducted by mail, telephone, the Internet (including but not limited to the world wide web, electronic mail and social media), business cards, signs, television, radio, magazines, newspapers, and telephonic greetings or answering machine messages.

B. (Repealed)

C. Prominent. "Prominent" means standing out so as to be seen easily; conspicuous; particularly noticeable.

2. (Repealed)

3. (Repealed)

4-A. Advertising by Real Estate Brokerage Agencies

Real estate brokerage advertisements must contain the trade name as licensed by the Commission of the real estate brokerage agency that placed the advertisement. The trade name of the agency must be prominently displayed or presented. In an advertisement that appears on or is sent via the Internet, the trade name of the agency that placed the advertisement must prominently appear or be readily accessible.

In addition, the designated broker may authorize an advertisement that includes the name, telephone number, slogan, logotype or photo of an affiliated licensee or group or team of affiliated licensees as part of the brokerage services being offered by the real estate brokerage agency. The affiliated licensee or group or team of affiliated licensees may not independently engage in real estate brokerage.

5. Written Permission of Owner Required to Advertise
A real estate brokerage agency or its affiliated licensees shall not advertise any real estate for sale without first obtaining the written permission of the owner or the owner's authorized representative.

6. Advertising of Exclusive Listing Held by Another Agency
A real estate brokerage agency or its affiliated licensees shall not publish or cause to be published an advertisement that makes reference to the availability of real estate which is exclusively listed for sale by another real estate brokerage agency unless the licensee obtains the prior written consent of the designated broker who has been authorized by the owner to provide consent.

7. Deception and Misrepresentation Prohibited
Advertising must be free from deception and shall not misrepresent the condition of the real estate, terms of the sale or purchase, real estate brokerage agency policies, or real estate brokerage services.

2. Acting in Self-Interest

A licensee holding an active real estate license shall disclose, in the offer to purchase, that the licensee is a real estate licensee:
1. When buying real estate not listed with a real estate brokerage agency;
2. When buying real estate listed with the licensee's real estate brokerage agency; or
3. When buying real estate and sharing in the brokerage fee resulting from the sale of such real estate.

3. Market Value

1. When Opinion Permitted
A licensee may provide a free opinion of value to a buyer or seller when the licensee is soliciting the buyer or seller to provide brokerage

services and before an agreement to provide any services has been reached or executed.

2. When Advice Prohibited

At any time after the solicitation to provide brokerage services, as described in Section 3(1) of this chapter, a transaction broker may not provide advice to either party regarding market value.

3. Provision of Comparable Market Data

A licensee who provides comparable market data to a buyer or seller for the buyer or seller to determine market value or list price is performing a ministerial act as defined in 32 MRSA §13271 (9).

4. Factors or Conditions That May Impact Client's Interest

A licensee who represents a buyer or seller client shall advise the client of any factors or conditions actually known by the licensee, or if acting in a reasonable manner, should have been known by the licensee, that may materially impact the client's interest as it pertains to the market value of real estate.

4. Net Listing Prohibited

A net listing shall be prohibited. A net listing is a type of listing in which the real estate brokerage agency receives, as commission, all excess money over and above the minimum sale price set by the seller.

5. Duty to Furnish Real Estate Brokerage-Related Documents

A licensee shall furnish copies of brokerage agreements, offers, counteroffers, and all types of contracts to all parties at the time of their signatures. Upon obtaining a written acceptance of an offer or counteroffer to purchase real estate, a licensee shall, within a reasonable time, deliver true, legible copies of the purchase and sale contract, signed by the seller and buyer, to both seller and buyer.

6. Disclosure of Real Estate Brokerage Agency Compensation Policy

1. Other Agencies

Written brokerage agreements must include a statement disclosing the real estate brokerage agency's policy on cooperating with and compensating other real estate brokerage agencies in the sale or purchase of real estate. If the real estate brokerage agency's policy is not to compensate all other real estate brokerage agencies in the same manner, this policy must be included in the statement and include a notice to the buyer or seller that this policy may limit the participation of other real estate brokerage agencies in the market-place.

2. Affiliated Licensees

When a real estate brokerage agency's policy on paying commis-sions to its affiliated licensees provides for an incentive to an affili-ated licensee for a greater commission for an in-house sale versus transactions involving a cooperating real estate brokerage agency, this policy must be disclosed in a written brokerage agreement with a buyer or seller.

7. Disclosed Dual Agency

A real estate brokerage agency which has a written company policy that permits disclosed dual agency shall obtain the informed written con-sent, as set forth in 32 MRSA §13275, of the seller or buyer to the dis-closed dual agency relationship at the time of entering into a written brokerage agreement that creates an agent-client relationship.

8. Appointed Agent Procedures and Disclosure

1. Designated Broker Responsibilities - Appointed Agent

A. A designated broker appointing an affiliated licensee(s) to act as an agent of a client shall take ordinary and necessary care to pro-tect confidential information disclosed by the client to the ap-pointed agent.

B. An appointed agent may disclose to the agency's designated bro-ker, or a designee specified by the designated broker, confiden-tial information of a client for the purpose of seeking advice or assistance for the benefit of the client in regard to a possible transaction. Confidential information shall be treated as such by the designated broker or other specified representative of the broker and shall not be disclosed unless otherwise required by 32 MRSA Chapter 114 or related rules or requested or permitted by the client who originally disclosed the confidential infor-mation.

C. A designated broker who is appointed to act as the agent of the client must select a designee to fulfill the responsibilities as listed in Section 8(1)(B) of this chapter.

2. Appointed Agent – Disclosure

The appointed agent disclosure shall be provided to the client prior to entering into a written brokerage agreement and shall include, at a minimum, the following provisions:

A. The name of the appointed agent and type of license held;

B. A statement that the appointed agent will be the client's agent and will owe the client fiduciary duties which, among other things, include the obligation not to reveal confidential information obtained from the client to other licensees, except to the designated broker or the designated broker's designee, as listed in Section 8(1)(B) of this chapter, for the purpose of seeking advice or assistance for the benefit of the client;

C. A statement that the real estate brokerage agency may be representing both the seller and the buyer in connection with the sale or purchase of real estate;

D. A statement that other agents may be appointed during the term of the written brokerage agreement should the appointed agent not be able to fulfill the terms of the written brokerage agreement or as by agreement between the designated broker and client. At the appointment of new or additional agent(s), the designated broker must comply with the provisions of this Section, including but not limited to, obtaining the client's signature consenting or not consenting to the appointment. An appointment of another agent as a new or additional agent does not relieve the first appointed agent of any of the fiduciary duties owed to the client; and

E. A section for the client to consent or not consent, in writing, to the appointment.

9. Real Estate Brokerage Relationship Disclosure Procedures

1. Real Estate Brokerage Relationships Form

The Commission incorporates into this chapter by reference the Real Estate Brokerage Relationships Form attached to this chapter. (Maine Real Estate Commission Form #3 revised 07/06).

2. Obligation to Furnish Real Estate Brokerage Relationships Form

Except as provided in Section 9(3) of this chapter, a licensee shall furnish a prospective buyer or seller with a copy of the Real Estate Brokerage Relationships Form when there is substantive communication regarding a real estate transaction by either a face-to-face meeting, a written communication, or an electronic communication with the prospective buyer or seller.

Exceptions

A licensee is not required to provide a copy of the form to a prospective buyer or seller in the following instances:

A. The real estate is land without a residential dwelling unit or is land with more than 4 residential dwelling units;
B. The licensee is acting solely as a principal in a real estate transaction;
C. The written communication from the licensee is a solicitation of business; or
D. The licensee has knowledge, or may reasonably assume, that another licensee has given a copy of the form to a prospective buyer or seller in that transaction.

4. Completion of Real Estate Brokerage Relationships Form
The licensee shall complete the appropriate section of the form relating to the presentation of the form.

10. Solicitation of Written Brokerage Agreements

A licensee shall not solicit a written brokerage agreement from a seller or buyer if the licensee knows, or acting in a reasonable manner should have known, that the buyer or seller has contracted with another real estate brokerage agency for the same real estate brokerage services on an exclusive basis. This Section does not preclude a real estate brokerage agency from entering into a written brokerage agreement with a seller or buyer, when the initial contact is initiated by the seller or buyer, provided that the written brokerage agreement does not become effective until the expiration or release of the previous written brokerage agreement.

11. Inducements

The offering of a free gift, prize, money or other valuable consideration by a real estate brokerage agency or affiliated licensee as an inducement shall be free from deception, and shall not serve to distort the true value of the real estate or the service being promoted. Any limitations or conditions of the offering must be prominently displayed or presented. In an offering that appears on or is sent via the Internet, any limitations or conditions of the offering must prominently appear in the offering itself, or in a page view or window that is directly and immediately accessible via a link in the offering. The link must be identified by words such as "limitations," "conditions," or "terms of offer" and must prominently appear in the offering.

12. Confidentiality of Offers and Purchase and Sale Contract Terms

During the pendency of the transaction, the real estate brokerage agency or affiliated licensee shall not disclose any terms of an offer, counteroffer or purchase and sale contract to anyone other than the buyer and seller without the prior written permission of the buyer and seller, except said documents shall be made available to the director of the Commission upon request.

13. Licensee's Duty

1. Keep the Designated Broker Informed

An affiliated licensee shall keep the designated broker fully informed of all activities conducted on behalf of the agency and shall notify the designated broker of any other activities that might impact on the re-sponsibilities of the designated broker as required under Chapter 400, Section 1 of the Commission's rules.

2 Provide Documents to Designated Broker

An affiliated licensee must provide originals or true copies of all real estate brokerage documents and records prepared in a real estate transaction and as listed in Chapter 400, Section 3 of the Commission's rules to the designated broker within 5 calendar days after execution of the document or record.

3. Domain Names and Web Sites

An affiliated licensee may not directly or indirectly, through himself or others—

- register a domain name for a web site, or
- develop or upload to the internet a web site,

that promotes real estate brokerage services or the sale or purchase or real estate through the agency with whom the licensee is affiliated without the consent of the designated broker. Any web site developed or uploaded under this Section must comply with the advertising re-quirements contained in Chapter 410, Section 1.

14. Licensee's Duty to Obtain and Provide Disclosure Information on Private Water Supply, Heating, Waste Disposal System and Known Hazardous Materials

1. Listing Licensee

A listing licensee shall be responsible for obtaining information neces-sary to make disclosures, as set forth in Sections 15 to 18 of this chapter, to buyers and shall make a reasonable effort to assure that the information is conveyed to a selling licensee.

2. Selling Licensee

A selling licensee shall be responsible for obtaining from the listing licensee the information necessary for making disclosures, as set forth in Sections 15 to 18 of this chapter, and for assuring that the disclosures are made to buyers.

3. Unlisted Property

A licensee shall be responsible for obtaining from the seller in a real estate brokerage transaction where the property is not listed with a real estate brokerage agency, the information necessary for making disclosures, as set forth in Sections 15 to 18 of this chapter, and for assuring that the disclosures are made to the buyer.

15. Private Water Supply Disclosure

A licensee listing a single-family residential property, a multifamily property, a residential lot or a commercial property with a residential component served by a private water supply, and a licensee in such transactions when the property is not listed with a real estate brokerage agency, shall ask the seller for the following information:

1. Type of system;
2. Location;
3. Malfunctions;
4. Date of installation;
5. Date of most recent water test; and
6. Whether or not the seller has experienced a problem such as an unsatisfactory water test or a water
7. test with notations.

Such information and any other information pertinent to the private water supply shall be conveyed, in writing, to a buyer prior to or during preparation of an offer. The fact that information regarding the private water supply is not available shall also be conveyed, in writing, when such is the case.

16. Heating Disclosure

A licensee listing a single-family residential property, a multifamily property or a commercial property with a residential component, and a licensee in such transactions when the property is not listed with a real estate brokerage agency, shall ask the seller for the following information regarding the heating system(s) and/or source(s):

1. Type(s);
2. Age of system/source(s);
3. Name of company who services system/source(s);
4. Date of most recent service call;
5. Annual consumption per system/source (i.e. gallons, kilowatt hours, cords);
6. Malfunctions per system/source within the past 2 years.

Such information and any other information pertinent to the heating system(s) and/or source(s) shall be conveyed, in writing, to a buyer prior to or during the preparation of an offer. The fact that information pertinent to the heating system(s) and/or source(s) is not available shall be conveyed, in writing, when such is the case.

17. Waste Disposal System Disclosure

1. Private Waste Disposal System

A licensee listing a single-family residential property, a multifamily property, a residential lot or a commercial property with a residential component served by a private waste disposal system, and a licensee in such transactions when the property is not listed with a real estate brokerage agency, shall ask the seller for the following information:

A. Type of system;
B. Size of tank;
C. Type of tank;
D. Location of tank;
E. Malfunctions of tank;
F. Date of installation of tank;
G. Location of leach field;
H. Malfunctions of leach field;
I. Date of installation of leach field;
J. Date of most recent servicing of system; and
K. Name of the contractor who services the system.

Such information and any other information pertinent to the waste disposal system shall be conveyed, in writing, to a buyer prior to or during preparation of an offer. The fact that information regarding the waste disposal system is not available shall also be conveyed, in writing, when such is the case.

2. Municipal or Quasi-Public Waste Disposal System

A licensee listing a single-family residential property, a multifamily property, a residential lot or a commercial property with a residential component served by a municipal or quasi-public waste disposal system, and a licensee in such transactions when the property is not listed with a real estate brokerage agency, shall ask the seller if the seller has experienced any system or line malfunction. This information shall be conveyed, in writing, to a buyer prior to or during the preparation of an offer.

18. Known Hazardous Materials Disclosure

1. Duty to Keep Informed

A licensee shall keep informed of any federal, state or local laws, rules, regulations or ordinances concerning known hazardous materials that may impact negatively upon the health and well being of buyers and sellers.

2. Duty to Disclose

A listing licensee, and a licensee in transactions when the property is not listed with a real estate brokerage agency, shall disclose, in writing, whether the seller makes any representations regarding current or previously existing known hazardous materials on or in the real estate. In addition, the licensee shall give a written statement to the buyer encouraging the buyer to seek information from professionals regarding any specific hazardous material issue or concern. Such written representation and statement shall be conveyed to a buyer prior to or during the preparation of an offer.

3. Request for Information From Seller

A licensee listing a single-family residential property, a multifamily property, a commercial property with a residential component and a licensee in such transactions when the property is not listed with a real estate brokerage agency, shall ask the seller whether the seller has any knowledge of current or previously existing asbestos, radon, lead based paint, and underground storage tanks. Such information and any other information pertinent to hazardous materials shall be conveyed, in writing, to a buyer prior to or during preparation of an offer. The fact that information regarding hazardous materials is not available shall also be conveyed, in writing, when such is the case.

19. Referral Fees

1. Certain Referral Fees Prohibited

A licensee may not receive compensation or other valuable considera-tion from a title company, lender or closing company or any affiliated employee for directing a buyer or seller in a real estate transaction to a company or an individual for financing, title or closing services.

2. Disclosure of Certain Referral Fees Required

A licensee who anticipates receiving compensation or other valuable consideration from a company or person for a referral of services, other than the services listed in Section 19(1) of this chapter or real estate brokerage services, to a buyer or seller during a real estate brokerage transaction may not accept such compensation or valuable considera-tion unless the licensee discloses in writing to the person paying for such service, and to the client if not the same person, that the licensee anticipates receiving such compensation or other valuable compensa-tion for such referral.

Maine Real Estate Relationships Brokerage Form

Dept. of Professional & Financial Regulation
Office of Professional & Occupational Regulation

MAINE REAL ESTATE COMMISSION

35 State House Station Augusta ME 04333-0035

REAL ESTATE BROKERAGE RELATIONSHIPS FORM

Right Now You Are A Customer

Are you interested in buying or selling residential real estate in Maine? Before you begin working with a real estate licensee it is important for you to understand that Maine Law provides for different levels of brokerage service to buyers and sellers. You should decide whether you want to be represented in a transaction (as a client) or not (as a customer). To assist you in deciding which option is in your best interest, please review the following information about real estate brokerage relationships.

Maine law requires all real estate brokerage companies and their affiliated licensees ("licensee") to perform certain basic duties when dealing with a buyer or seller. You can expect a real estate licensee you deal with to provide the following **customer-level services:**

√ To disclose all material defects pertaining to the physical condition of the real estate that are known by the licensee;

√ To treat both the buyer and seller honestly and not knowingly give false information;

√ To account for all money and property received from or on behalf of the buyer or seller; and

√ To comply with all state and federal laws related to real estate brokerage activity.

Until you enter into a written brokerage agreement with the licensee for client-level representation you are considered a "customer" and the licensee is not your agent. **As a customer, you should not expect the licensee to promote your best interest, or to keep any information you give to the licensee confidential, including your bargaining position.**

You May Become A Client

If you want a licensee to represent you, you will need to enter into a written listing agreement or a written buyer representation agreement. These agreements **create a client-agent relationship** between you and the licensee. As a client you can expect the licensee to provide the following services. **In addition to** the basic services required of all licensees listed above:

√ To perform the terms of the written agreement with skill and care;

√ To promote your best interests;

- For seller clients this means the agent will put the seller's interests first and negotiate the best price and terms for the seller;

- For buyer clients this means the agent will put the buyer's interests first and negotiate for the best prices and terms for the buyer; and

√ To maintain the confidentiality of specific client information, including bargaining information.

COMPANY POLICY ON CLIENT-LEVEL SERVICES — WHAT YOU NEED TO KNOW

The real estate brokerage company's policy on client-level services determines which of the three types of agent-client relationships permitted in Maine may be offered to you. The agent-client relationships permitted in Maine are as follows:

√ The company and all of its affiliated licensees represent you as a client (called "**single agency**");

√ The company appoints, with your written consent, one or more of the affiliated licensees to represent you as an agent(s) (called "**appointed agency**");

√ The company may offer limited agent level services as a **disclosed dual agent**.

WHAT IS A DISCLOSED DUAL AGENT?

In certain situations a licensee may act as an agent for and represent both the buyer and the seller in the same transaction. This is called **disclosed dual agency**. *Both the buyer and the seller must consent to this type of representation in writing.*

Working with a dual agent is not the same as having your own exclusive agent as a single or appointed agent. For instance, when representing both a buyer and a seller, the dual agent must not disclose to one party any confidential information obtained from the other party.

Remember!

Unless you enter into a written agreement for agency representation, you are a customer—not a client.

THIS IS NOT A CONTRACT

It is important for you to know that this form is not a contract. The licensee's completion of the statement below acknowledges that you have been given the information required by Maine law regarding brokerage relationships so that you may make an informed decision as to the relationship you wish to establish with the licensee/company.

To Be Completed By Licensee

This form was presented on (date)_____

To_____
Name of Buyer(s) or Seller(s)

by_____
Licensee's Name

on behalf of_____
Company/Agency

MREC Form#3 Revised 07/2006
Office Title Changed 09/2011

To check on the license status of the real estate brokerage company or affiliated licensee go to www.maine.gov/professionallicensing. Inactive licensees may not practice real estate brokerage.

MAINE REVISED STATUTE TITLE 32, CHAPTER 124:
REAL ESTATE APPRAISAL LICENSING AND CERTIFICATION

§14003. LICENSE REQUIRED

Except as provided in section 14004, it is unlawful for a person to prepare, for a fee or other valuable consideration, an appraisal or appraisal report relating to real estate or real property in this State without first obtaining a real estate appraisal license. Only an individual may be licensed under this chapter. This section does not apply to individuals who do not render significant professional assistance in arriving at a real estate appraisal analysis, opinion or conclusion. Nothing in this chapter prohibits any person who is licensed to practice in this State under any other law from engaging in the practice for which that person is licensed.

§14004. EXEMPTION

Real estate appraisal activity does not include:

1. Salaried employees.

Appraisals prepared by a salaried employee of a real estate owner who, in the regular course of employment, makes appraisals of the real estate of the employer or of real estate under consideration for purchase or exchange for the sole consideration of the employer; and

2. Brokers or associate brokers.

Appraisals or opinions of market value prepared by associate brokers or brokers who maintain active licenses pursuant to chapter 114 rendered for purposes other than for federally related transactions.

Any opinion or appraisal of market value rendered under this section must contain the following language in bold print in a prominent location: "This opinion or appraisal was prepared solely for the client, for the purpose and function stated in this report and is not intended for subsequent use. It was not prepared by a licensed or certified appraiser and may not comply with the appraisal standards of the uniform standards of professional appraisal practice."

NOTE This an excerpt and not the complete chapter.

MAINE REVISED STATUTE TITLE 5, CHAPTER 341:

OCCUPATIONAL LICENSE DISQUALIFICATION ON BASIS OF CRIMINAL RECORD

§5301. ELIGIBILITY FOR OCCUPATIONAL LICENSE, REGISTRATION OR PERMIT

1. **Effect of criminal history record information respecting certain convictions.** Subject to subsection 2 and sections 5302 and 5303, in determining eligibility for the granting of any occupational license, registration or permit issued by the State, the appropriate State licensing agency may take into consideration criminal history record information from Maine or elsewhere relating to certain convictions which have not been set aside or for which a full and free pardon has not been granted, but the existence of such information shall not operate as an automatic bar to being licensed, registered or permitted to practice any profession, trade or occupation.

2. **Criminal history record information which may be considered.** A licensing agency may use in connection with an application for an occupational license, registration or permit criminal history record information pertaining to the following:

   A. Convictions for which incarceration for less than one year may be imposed and which involve dishonesty or false statement;

   B. Convictions for which incarceration for less than one year may be imposed and which directly relate to the trade or occupation for which the license or permit is sought;

   C. Convictions for which no incarceration can be imposed and which directly relate to the trade or occupation for which the license or permit is sought;

   D. Convictions for which incarceration for one year or more may be imposed; or

   E. Convictions for which incarceration for less than one year may be imposed and that involve sexual misconduct by an applicant for massage therapy licensure or a licensed massage therapist or an applicant or licensee of the Board of Licensure in Medicine, the Board of Osteopathic Licensure, the Board of Dental Examiners, the State Board of Examiners of Psychologists, the State Board of Social Worker Licensure, the Board of Chiropractic Licensure, the State Board of Examiners in Physical Therapy, the State Board of Alcohol and Drug Counselors, the Board of Respiratory Care Practitioners, the Board of Counseling Professionals Licensure, the Board of Occupational Therapy Practice, the Board of Speech, Audiology and Hearing, the Radiologic Technology Board of Examiners, the Nursing Home Administrators Licensing Board, the Board of Licensure of Podiatric Medicine, the Board of Complementary Health Care Providers, the Maine Board of Pharmacy, the Board of Trustees of the Maine Criminal Justice Academy, the State Board of Nursing and the Emergency Medical Services' Board

§5302. DENIAL, SUSPENSION, REVOCATION OR OTHER DISCIPLINE OF LICENSEES BECAUSE OF CRIMINAL RECORD

1. **Reasons for disciplinary action.** Licensing agencies may refuse to grant or renew, or may suspend, revoke or take other disciplinary action against any occupational license, registration or permit on the basis of the criminal history record information relating to convictions denominated in section 5301, subsection 2, but only if the licensing agency determines that the applicant, licensee, registrant or permit holder so convicted has not been sufficiently rehabilitated to warrant the public trust. The applicant, licensee, registrant or permit holder shall bear the burden of proof that there exists sufficient rehabilitation to warrant the public trust.

2. **Reasons to be stated in writing**. The licensing agency shall explicitly state in writing the reasons for a decision which prohibits the applicant, licensee, registrant or permit holder from practicing the profession, trade or occupation if that decision is based in whole or in part on conviction of any crime described in section 5301, subsection 2.

§5303. TIME LIMIT ON CONSIDERATION OF PRIOR CRIMINAL CONVICTION

1. **Three-year limits**. Except as set forth in this subsection and subsection 2, the procedures outlined in sections 5301 and 5302 for the consideration of prior criminal conviction as an element of fitness to practice a licensed profession, trade or occupation shall apply within 3 years of the applicant's or licensee's final discharge, if any, from the correctional system. Beyond the 3-year period, ex-offender applicants or licensees with no additional convictions are to be considered in the same manner as applicants or licensees possessing no prior criminal record for the

purposes of licensing decisions. There is no time limitation for consideration of an applicant's or licensee's conduct which gave rise to the criminal conviction if that conduct is otherwise a ground for disciplinary action against a licensee

2. **Ten year limits.** For applicants to and licensees and registrants of the Board of Licensure in Medicine, the Board of Osteopathic Licensure, the Board of Dental Examiners, the State Board of Examiners of Psychologists, the State Board of Social Worker Licensure, the State Board of Nursing, the Board of Chiropractic Licensure, the Board of Trustees of the Maine Criminal Justice Academy, the State Board of Examiners in Physical Therapy, the State Board of Alcohol and Drug Counselors, the Board of Respiratory Care Practitioners, the Board of Counseling Professionals Licensure, the Board of Occupational Therapy Practice, the Board on Speech-language Pathology, Audiology and Hearing Aid Dealing and Fitting, the Radiologic Technology Board of Examiners, the Nursing Home Administrators Licensing Board, the Board of Licensure of Podiatric Medicine, the Board of Complementary Health Care Providers, the Maine Board of Pharmacy, and the Emergency Medical Services' Board and applicants for massage therapy licensure or licensed massage therapists, the following apply.

A. The procedures outlined in sections 5301 and 5302 for the consideration of prior criminal conviction as an element of fitness to practice a licensed profession, trade or occupation apply within 10 years of the applicant's or licensee's final discharge, if any, from the correctional system.

B. Beyond the 10-year period, ex-offender applicants or licensees with no additional convictions must be considered in the same manner as applicants or licensees possessing no prior criminal record for the purposes of licensing decisions.

C. There is no time limitation for consideration of a registrant's, an applicant's or licensee's conduct that gave rise to the criminal conviction if that conduct is otherwise a ground for disciplinary action.

§5304. APPEALS

Any person who is aggrieved by the decision of any licensing agency in possible violation of this chapter may file a statement of complaint with the District Court designated in chapter 375.

MAINE REVISED STATUTE TITLE 10:

COMMERCE AND TRADE
Part 9: DEPARTMENT OF PROFESSIONAL AND FINANCIAL REGULATION
Chapter 901: DEPARTMENT OF BUSINESS REGULATION
(excerpts)

§8001. DEPARTMENT; ORGANIZATION

There is created and established the Department of Professional and Financial Regulation, in this chapter referred to as the "department," to regulate financial institutions, insurance companies, grantors of consumer credit and to license and regulate professions and occupations. The mission of the department is to encourage sound, ethical business practices through high-quality, impartial and efficient regulation of insurers, financial institutions, creditors, investment providers and numerous professions and occupations for the purpose of protecting consumers. The department is composed of the following:

1. **Bureau of Financial Institutions. Bureau of Financial Institutions**;
2. **Bureau of Consumer Credit Protection. Bureau of Consumer Credit Protection**;
3. **Bureau of Insurance. Bureau of Insurance**;
3-A. **Office of Securities. Office of Securities; and**
38. **Office of Professional and Occupational Regulation.** The Office of Professional and Occupational Regulation also administers the following regulatory functions: licensure of athletic trainers; licensure of massage therapists; licensure of interpreters for the deaf and hard-of-hearing; licensure of persons pursuant to the Charitable Solicitations Act; and licensure of transient sellers, including door-to-door home repair transient sellers.

Office of Professional and Occupational Regulation.
The Office of Professional and Occupational Regulation is composed of the following:
   A. Board of Accountancy;
   D. Maine State Board for Licensure of Architects, Landscape Architects and Interior Designers;
   E. Maine Athletic Commission;

F. Board of Licensing of Auctioneers;

G. Repealed

H. Board of Chiropractic Licensure;

H-1. Board of Complementary Health Care Providers;

I. Board of Driver Education;

J. Board of Counseling Professionals Licensure;

K. Board of Licensing of Dietetic Practice;

L. Electricians' Examining Board;

M. Board of Licensure of Foresters;

N. State Board of Funeral Service;

O. State Board of Certification for Geologists and Soil Scientists;

P. Repealed

Q. Board of Licensure for Professional Land Surveyors;

R. Manufactured Housing Board;

§8002. DUTIES AND AUTHORITY OF COMMISSIONER

The Commissioner of Professional and Financial Regulation, referred to in this chapter as the "commissioner," is the chief administrative officer of the department and is responsible for supervising the administration of the department. The commissioner is appointed by the Governor, subject to review by the joint standing committee of the Legislature having jurisdiction over banking and insurance matters, and to confirmation by the Legislature. In making the appointment under this paragraph, the Governor shall appoint one of the following officials as commissioner, who shall also continue to act as a superintendent or director, as the case may be: the Superintendent of Financial Institutions, the Superintendent of Consumer Credit Protection, the Superintendent of Insurance or the Director of the Office of Licensing and Registration. The commissioner serves at the pleasure of the Governor. Unless otherwise provided in law, the commissioner may not exercise or interfere with the exercise of discretionary regulatory authority granted by statute to the bureaus, offices, boards or commissions within and affiliated with the department. As chief administrative officer of the department, the commissioner has the following duties and authority to:

1. **Budget.** Prepare the budget for the department;

2. **Personnel.** Except as otherwise specified, appoint and remove, subject to the Civil Service Law, all personnel considered necessary to fulfill the duties and functions of the department; appoint an assistant to the commissioner to serve at the commissioner's pleasure;

and transfer personnel within the department to ensure efficient utilization of department personnel;

3. **Purchases.** Coordinate the purchase and use of all equipment and supplies within the department;

4. **Review.** Review the organization, functions and operation of bureaus, offices, boards and commissions within and affiliated with the department to ensure that overlapping functions and operations are eliminated and that each complies fully with its statutory and public service responsibilities;

5. **Liaison.** Act as a liaison among the bureaus, offices, boards and commissions within and affiliated with the department and act as liaison between them and the Governor;

6. **Recommendations.** Recommend to the Governor and Legislature those changes in the laws relating to the organization, functions, services or procedures of the bureaus, offices, boards and commissions of the department as the commissioner determines desirable;

7. **Delegate authority.** Authorize the heads of bureaus, offices, boards and commissions within the department to carry out the commissioner's duties and authority;

8. **Adequate resources.** Ensure that each bureau, office, board and commission has adequate resources to carry out regulatory functions and that the department's expenditures are equitably apportioned;

9. **Licensing.** Coordinate all administrative processes related to licensing functions of bureaus, offices, boards and commissions within the department, including but not limited to the frequency and form of applications and licenses;

10. **Confidentiality of shared information.** Keep confidential any information provided by or to the commissioner that has been designated confidential by the agency, bureau, board or commission within or affiliated with the department that furnished the information and that is the property of the agency, bureau, board or commission that furnished the information. Any information provided pursuant to this subsection may not be disclosed by the recipient of the information unless disclosure has been authorized by the agency, bureau, board or commission that furnished the information; and

11. **Report on fees.** By December 1st of each even-numbered year, conduct a review of the fees assessed by the department and provide a written report to the State Budget Officer and the joint

standing committees of the Legislature having jurisdiction over appropriations and financial affairs, insurance and financial services matters and business, research and economic development matters identifying any fee changes the commissioner recommends for the next biennium.

12. **Recommend measures.** Recommend legislation or other measures to the Governor and the Legislature for the purpose of assisting current and former members of the United States Armed Forces in obtaining any professional license within the provisions of the department related to their relevant training and experience from their military service.

§8003. DEPARTMENTAL ORGANIZATION; DUTIES

1. **Division of Administrative Services.** There is created a Division of Administrative Services, which is a division within the department under the commissioner's office, to provide assistance to the commissioner and to the agencies within and affiliated with the department in civil service matters, budgeting and financial matters, purchasing, and clerical and support services, and to perform other duties the commissioner designates. The commissioner may employ a Director of Administrative Services and clerical and technical assistants necessary to discharge the duties of the division and shall outline their duties and fix their compensation, subject to the Civil Service Law.

A. Within the Division of Administrative Services, there is a computer services section. It is the responsibility of the computer services section to provide technical assistance to the Office of Licensing and Registration to process and issue original and renewal licenses for the department and for bureaus, offices, boards and commissions within the department as the commissioner directs. The licenses may be processed and issued only upon authorization of the appropriate bureau, office, board or commission or upon the authorization of the commissioner in the case of licenses granted directly by the department. The computer services section shall maintain a central register containing the name and address of each person or firm licensed by profession, occupation or industry and such other information as the commissioner may direct for administration, information or planning purposes. The commissioner, with the advice of the respective bureaus, offices, boards and commissions, may determine the type and form of licenses issued by all agencies within the department. The computer services section shall perform such other administrative services for the agencies within the department as the commissioner directs.

2. Office of Licensing and Registration.

2-A. Office of Professional and Occupational Regulation. There is created an Office of Licensing and Registration, referred to in this subsection as the "office," composed of the boards, commissions and regulatory functions set forth in section 8001, subsection 38. The commissioner may appoint a Director of the Office of Professional and Occupational Regulation and those clerical and technical assistants who are necessary to discharge the duties of the office and shall outline their duties and fix their compensation, subject to the Civil Service Law. Notwithstanding any other provision of law granting authority to a board or commission, the Director of the Office of Professional and Occupational Regulation has the following superseding powers, duties and functions:

A. To administer the office and maximize and direct the use of personnel and financial resources to regulate professionals in the best interest of the public;

B. To prepare and administer, with the advice of the boards and commissions, budgets necessary to carry out the regulatory purposes of the boards and commissions. The Director of the Office of Professional

C. To provide all staffing necessary and appropriate to administer the office and carry out the statutory missions of the boards, commissions and regulatory functions. All clerks, technical support staff and supervisors must be assigned to the office and allocated by the director to perform functions on behalf of the various boards, commissions and regulatory functions according to need;

D. To establish by rule and after reasonable notice to the affected board all fees necessary and appropriate for all boards, commissions and regulatory functions within the office, subject to any fee cap established by statute and applicable to that board, commission or regulatory function. The Director of the Office of Professional and Occupational Regulation shall set the criteria for all fees. The criteria must include, but are not limited to, the costs, statutory requirements, enforcement requirements and fees and expenses of each board, commission or regulatory function. Rules adopted pursuant to this paragraph are routine technical rules pursuant to Title 5, chapter 375, subchapter II-A;

E. To establish by rule, such processes and procedures necessary to administer the various boards, commissions and regulatory functions of the office, including, but not limited to, a uniform complaint procedure, a uniform procedure regarding protested checks, a uniform policy regarding the treatment of late renewals and a uniform procedure for substantiating continuing education requirements. Rules adopted pursuant to this paragraph are routine technical rules pursuant to Title 5, chapter 375, subchapter II-A;

F. To keep records of public meetings, proceedings and actions and to make those records available to the public at cost upon request, unless otherwise prohibited by state or federal law;

G. To enter into contracts to ensure the provision of goods and services necessary to perform regulatory functions and to fulfill statutory responsibilities. This authority includes the ability to employ and engage experts, professionals or other personnel of other state or federal regulatory agencies as necessary to assist the office in carrying out its regulatory functions and to contract office staff to other state and federal regulatory agencies to assist those agencies in carrying out their regulatory functions;

H. To perform licensing functions for other state agencies on a fee-for-service basis;

I. To enter into cooperative agreements with other state, federal or foreign regulatory agencies to facilitate the regulatory functions of the office, including, but not limited to, information sharing, coordination of examinations or inspections and joint examinations or inspections. Any information furnished pursuant to this paragraph by or to the office that has been designated confidential by the agency furnishing the information remains confidential and the property of the agency furnishing the information and may not be disclosed by the recipient of the information unless disclosure has been authorized by the agency that furnished the information;

J. To direct staff to review and approve applications for licensure or renewal in accordance with criteria established in statute or in rules adopted by a board or commission. Licensing decisions made by staff may be appealed to the full board or commission;

K. To prepare and submit to the commissioner an annual report of the office's operations, activities and goals; and

L. To study jurisdictional overlap between the department's boards and commissions and other state agencies for purposes of streamlining and consolidating related legal authorities and administrative processes.

3. License defined. For purposes of this section, the term "license" means a license, certification, registration, permit, approval or other similar document evidencing admission to or granting authority to engage in a profession, occupation, business or industry but does not mean a registration, permit, approval or similar document evidencing the granting of authority to engage in the business of banking pursuant to

4. Licensing periods; renewal dates. The commissioner may establish expiration or renewal dates and establish whether licenses are issued annually or biennially for all licenses authorized to be issued by bureaus, offices, boards and commissions within the department, notwithstanding any other provisions of law. If an expiration or renewal date established by the commissioner has the effect of shortening the term of a license currently in effect, the bureau, office, board or commission, or the department in the case of a license that it issues directly, shall credit the fee paid, on a prorated basis, for the unexpired term of the current license toward the renewal fee of the renewal license. If a license is not renewed on the new expiration or renewal date established by the commissioner, the license remains in effect through its original term, unless suspended or revoked sooner under laws or regulations of the respective bureau, office, board or commission. Should a licensee seek to renew the license at the end of the original term, the law or regulations established by the respective bureau, office, board or commission for late renewals or re-registrations apply. For the purpose of implementing and administering biennial licensing, the commissioner may permit bureaus, offices, boards and commissions within the department to issue licenses and establish renewal fees for less than a 2-year term. This section may not change the term or fee for one-time licenses, except as specifically stated.

4-A. Disclosure and recording of social security numbers. An individual who applies for a license shall provide that individual's social security number on the application, which must be recorded.

5-A. Authority of Office of Professional and Occupational Regulation. In addition to authority otherwise conferred, unless expressly precluded by language of denial in its own governing law, Office of Professional and Occupational Regulation, referred to in this subsection as "the office," including the licensing boards and commissions and regulatory functions within the office, have the following authority.

A. The office, board or commission may deny or refuse to renew a license, may suspend or revoke a license and may impose other discipline as authorized in this subsection for any of the following reasons:

    (1) The practice of fraud, deceit or misrepresentation in obtaining a license from a bureau, office, board or commission, or in connection with services rendered while engaged in the occupation or profession for which the person is licensed;

    (2) Any gross negligence, incompetence, misconduct or violation of an applicable code of ethics or standard of practice while engaged in the occupation or profession for which the person is licensed;

    (3) Subject to the limitations of Title 5, chapter 341, conviction of a Class A, B or C crime or of a crime that bears directly on the licensed profession or occupation;

    (4) Any violation of the governing law of an office, board or commission;

    (5) Any violation of the rules of an office, board or commission;

    (6) Engaging in any activity requiring a license under the governing law of an office, board or commission that is beyond the scope of acts authorized by the license held;

    (7) Continuing to act in a capacity requiring a license under the governing law of an office, board or commission after expiration, suspension or revocation of that license;

    (8) Aiding or abetting unlicensed practice by a person who is not licensed as required by the governing law of an office, board or commission;

    (9) Noncompliance with an order or consent agreement of an office, board or commission;

    (10) Failure to produce any requested documents in the licensee's possession or under the licensee's control concerning a pending complaint or proceeding or any matter under investigation; or

    (11) Any violation of a requirement imposed pursuant to

section 8003-G.

B. The office, board or commission may impose the following forms of discipline upon a licensee or applicant for licensure:

(1) Denial or refusal to renew a license, or issuance of a license in conjunction with the imposition of other discipline;

(2) Issuance of warning, censure or reprimand. Each warning, censure or reprimand issued must be based upon violation of a single applicable law, rules or condition of licensure or must be based upon a single instance of actionable conduct or activity;

(3) Suspension of a license for up to 90 days for each violation of applicable laws, rules or conditions of licensure or for each instance of actionable conduct or activity. Suspensions may be set to run concurrently or consecutively. Execution of all or any portion of a term of suspension may be stayed pending successful completion of conditions of probation, although the suspension remains part of the licensee's record;

(4) Revocation of a license;

(5) Imposition of civil penalties of up to $1,500, or such greater amount as may be authorized by statute, for each violation of applicable laws, rules or conditions of licensure or for each instance of actionable conduct or activity;

(6) Imposition of conditions of probation upon an applicant or licensee. Probation may run for such time period as the office, board or commission determines appropriate. Probation may include conditions such as: additional continuing education; medical, psychiatric or mental health consultations or evaluations; mandatory professional or occupational supervision of the applicant or licensee; practice restrictions; and other conditions as the office, board or commission determines appropriate. Costs incurred in the performance of terms of probation are borne by the applicant or licensee. Failure to comply with the conditions of probation is a ground for disciplinary action against a licensee.

C. The office, board or commission may execute a consent agreement that resolves a complaint or investigation without further proceedings. Consent agreements may be entered into only with the consent of the applicant or licensee; the office, board or commission; and the Department of the Attorney General. Any remedy, penalty or fine that is otherwise available by law, even if only in the jurisdiction of the Superior Court, may be achieved by consent agreement, including long-term suspension and permanent revocation of a professional or occupational license. A consent agreement is not subject to review or appeal and may be modified only by a writing executed by all parties to the original consent agreement. A consent agreement is enforceable by an action in Superior Court.

D. The office, board or commission may:

(3) Except as provided in Title 37-B, section 390-A, adopt rules requiring continuing professional or occupational education and require applicants for license renewal to present proof of satisfactory completion of continuing professional or occupational education in accordance with such rules. Failure to comply with the continuing education rules is punishable by nonrenewal of the license and other discipline authorized by this subsection. Notwithstanding any contrary provision set forth in the governing law of an office, board or commission, continuing education requirements may coincide with the license renewal period. Rules adopted pursuant to this subparagraph are routine technical rules as described in Title 5, chapter 375, subchapter 2-A;

(4) Issue continuing education deferments in cases of undue hardship;

(5) Grant inactive status licenses to licensees in accordance with rules that may be adopted by each office, board or commission. The fee for an inactive status license may not exceed the statutory fee cap for license renewal set forth in the governing law of the office, board or commission. Licensees in inactive status are required to pay license renewal fees for renewal of an inactive status license and may be required to pay a reinstatement fee as set by the Director of the Office of Licensing and Registration if the license is reactivated on a date other than the ordinary renewal date of the license. Any rules of an office, board or commission regulating inactive status licensure must describe the obligations of an inactive status licensee with respect to any ongoing continuing education requirement in effect for licensees of the office, board or commission and must set forth any requirements for reinstatement to active status, which requirements may include continuing education. Rules adopted pursuant to this subparagraph are routine technical rules as described in Title 5, chapter 375, subchapter 2-A; and

(6) Delegate to staff the authority to review and approve applications for licensure pursuant to procedures and criteria established by rule. Rules adopted pursuant to this subparagraph are routine technical rules as described in Title 5, chapter 375, subchapter 2-A.

E. The office, board or commission may require surrender of licenses. In order for a licensee's surrender of a license to be effective, a surrender must first be accepted by vote of the office, board or commission. The office, board or commission may refuse to accept surrender of a license if the licensee is under investigation or is the subject of a pending complaint or proceeding, unless a consent agreement is first entered into pursuant to this subsection. The consent agreement may include terms and conditions for reinstatement.

F. The office, board or commission may issue a letter of guidance or concern to a licensee. A letter of guidance or concern may be used to educate, reinforce knowledge regarding legal or professional obligations or express concern over action or inaction by the licensee that does not rise to the level of misconduct sufficient to merit disciplinary action. The issuance of a letter of guidance or concern is not a formal proceeding and does not constitute an adverse disciplinary action of any form. Notwithstanding any other provision of law, letters of guidance or concern are not confidential. The office, board or commission may place letters of guidance or concern, together with any underlying complaint, report and investigation materials, in a licensee's file for a specified period of time, not to exceed 10 years. Any letters, complaints and materials placed on file may be accessed and considered by the office, board or commission in any subsequent action commenced against the licensee within the specified time frame. Complaints, reports and investigation materials placed on file are confidential only to the extent that confidentiality is required pursuant to Title 24, chapter 21.

G. The office, board or commission may establish, by rule, procedures for licensees in another state to be licensed in this State by written agreement with another state, by entering into written licensing compacts with other states or by any other method of license recognition considered appropriate that ensures the health, safety and welfare of the public. Rules adopted pursuant to this paragraph are routine technical rules pursuant to Title 5, chapter 375, subchapter 2-A.

The jurisdiction to suspend and revoke occupational and professional licenses conferred by this subsection is concurrent with that of the District Court. Civil penalties must be paid to the Treasurer of State.

Any nonconsensual disciplinary action taken under authority of this subsection other than denial or nonrenewal of a license may be imposed only after a hearing conforming to the requirements of Title 5, chapter 375, subchapter 4, and, except for revocation actions, is subject to judicial review exclusively in the Superior Court in accordance with Title 5, chapter 375, subchapter 7.

The office, board or commission shall hold a hearing conforming to the requirements of Title 5, chapter 375, subchapter 4 at the written request of any person who is denied an initial or renewal license without a hearing for any reason other than failure to pay a fee, provided that the request for hearing is received by the office, board or commission within 30 days of the applicant's receipt of written notice of the denial of the application, the reasons for the denial and the applicant's right to request a hearing.

The office, board or commission may subpoena witnesses, records and documents in any adjudicatory hearing it conducts.

Rules adopted to govern judicial appeals from agency action apply to cases brought under this subsection.

In the event of appeal to Superior Court from any form of discipline imposed pursuant to this subsection, including denial or nonrenewal of a license, the office, board or commission may assess the licensed person or entity for the costs of transcribing and reproducing the administrative record.

6. **Funding.** The commissioner may assess each internal bureau, office, board or commission served by the commissioner's office, the Division of Administrative Services or the Office of Licensing and Registration its reasonable share of an amount sufficient to cover the cost of operating those service agencies. The commissioner may assess any board affiliated with the department for the services the board receives from the department. The commissioner may assess other state agencies for licensing functions performed on behalf of those agencies by the Office of Licensing and Registration.

7. **Evidentiary effect of certificate.** Notwithstanding any provision of law or rule of evidence, the certificate of the commissioner under

the seal of the State must be received by any court in this State as prima facie evidence of the issuance, suspension or revocation of any license issued by the department.

8. **Display of license.**
9. **Construction.**
10. **National disciplinary record system.** Within the limits of available revenues, all bureaus, offices, boards or commissions internal or affiliated with the department shall join or subscribe to a national disciplinary record system used to track interstate movement of regulated professionals who have been the subject of discipline by state boards, commissions or agencies and report disciplinary actions taken within this State to that system.

§8003-A. COMPLAINT INVESTIGATION

1. **Affiliated boards.** In aid of their investigative authority, the licensing boards and commissions affiliated with the department pursuant to section 8001-A may issue subpoenas in the name of the relevant licensing board or commission, in accordance with the terms of Title 5, section 9060, except that the authority applies to any stage of an investigation and is not limited to an adjudicatory proceeding.
2. **Office of Professional and Occupational Regulation.** The Office of Professional and Occupational Regulation, including the licensing boards and commissions and regulatory functions within the office, may receive, initiate and investigate complaints alleging any ground for disciplinary action set forth in section 8003, subsection 5-A. To assist with complaint or other investigations, or as otherwise considered necessary for the fulfillment of their responsibilities, the office, boards and commissions may hold hearings and may issue subpoenas for witnesses, records and documents in the name of the office, board or commission, as the case may be, in accordance with the terms of Title 5, section 9060, except that the subpoena authority applies to any stage or type of an investigation and is not limited to an adjudicatory hearing held pursuant to section 8003, subsection 5-A.

Investigative personnel of the Office of Professional and Occupational Regulation, during the normal conduct of their work for boards, commissions and regulatory functions within the office, may conduct investigations, issue citations, serve summonses and order corrections of violations in accordance with specific statutory authority. When specific authority does not exist to appeal an order to correct, that process must be established by rule by the respective board.

3. **Dispositions available to the public.** Upon disposition of each complaint and investigation, the office and all boards and commissions shall make such disposition available to the public.

§8003-B. CONFIDENTIALITY OF INVESTIGATIVE RECORDS

1. **During investigation.** Unless otherwise provided by Title 24, chapter 21, all complaints and investigative records of the licensing boards and commissions within or affiliated with the Department of Professional and Financial Regulation are confidential during the pendency of an investigation. Those records become public records upon the conclusion of an investigation unless confidentiality is required by some other provision of law. For purposes of this section, an investigation is concluded when:

A. A notice of an adjudicatory hearing under Title 5, chapter 375, subchapter IV has been issued;

B. [1999, c. 687, Pt. C, §10 (RP).]

C. A consent agreement has been executed; or

D. A letter of dismissal has been issued or the investigation has otherwise been closed.

2. **Exceptions.** Notwithstanding subsection 1, during the pendency of an investigation, a complaint or investigative record may be disclosed:

A. To department employees designated by the commissioner;

B. To designated complaint officers of the appropriate board or commission;

C. By a department employee or complaint officer designated by the commissioner when, and to the extent, deemed necessary to facilitate the investigation;

D. To other state or federal agencies when the files contain evidence of possible violations of laws enforced by those agencies;

E. When, and to the extent, deemed necessary by the commissioner to avoid imminent and serious harm. The authority of the commissioner to make such a disclosure shall not be delegated;

F. Pursuant to rules which shall be promulgated by the department, when it is determined that confidentiality is no longer warranted due to general public knowledge of the circumstances surrounding the complaint or investigation and when the investigation would not be prejudiced by the disclosure;

and

G. To the person investigated on request. The commissioner may refuse to disclose part or all of any investigative information, including the fact of an investigation, when the commissioner determines that disclosure would prejudice the investigation. The authority of the commissioner to make such a determination shall not be delegated.

2-A. Certain client records confidential. Notwithstanding subsections 1 and 2, a treatment record provided to a licensing board or commission within or affiliated with the department during investigation of a person licensed by the department in a medical, mental health, substance abuse, psychological or health field that contains information personally identifying a licensee's client or patient is confidential during the pendency of the investigation and remains confidential upon the conclusion of the investigation. A treatment record may be disclosed only if:

A. The client or patient executes a written release that states that:

(1) Unless the release provides for more limited disclosure, execution of the release may result in the record becoming a public record; or

(2) If the client or patient wishes, execution of the release allows disclosure to only the person or persons clearly identified in the release. The release must require the person or persons identified in the release not to make a disclosure to another person;

B. The disclosure is necessary under Title 22, chapter 857 concerning personnel and licensure actions;

C. The disclosure is necessary under Title 22, section 3474 concerning reports of suspected adult abuse or exploitation;

D. The disclosure is necessary under Title 22, section 4011-A concerning reports of suspected child abuse or neglect; or

E. The disclosure is necessary under Title 22, section 7703 concerning reports of suspected child or adult abuse or neglect.

A release executed by a client or patient does not operate to disclose a record otherwise made confidential by law.

This subsection does not prevent disclosure of records pursuant to an order of a court of competent jurisdiction upon good cause shown.

3. Attorney General records. The provision or disclosure of investigative records of the Department of the Attorney General to a departmental employee designated by the commissioner or to a complaint officer of a board or commission does not constitute a waiver of the confidentiality of those records for any other purposes. Further disclosure of those investigative records is subject to Title 16, section 804 and the discretion of the Attorney General.

4. **Violation.** A person who knowingly or intentionally makes a disclosure in violation of this section or who knowingly violates a condition of a release pursuant to subsection 2-A commits a civil violation for which a forfeiture not to exceed $1,000 may be adjudged.

§8003-C. UNLICENSED PRACTICE

1. **Complaints of unlicensed practice.** A board or commission listed in section 8001, subsection 38 or section 8001-A or a regulatory function administered by the Office of Professional and Occupational Regulation identified in section 8001, subsection 38 may receive or initiate complaints of unlicensed practice.

2. **Investigation of unlicensed practice.** Complaints or allegations of unlicensed practice may be investigated by the Office of Professional and Occupational Regulation, the Attorney General's office or a board's or commission's complaint officer or inspector. If sufficient evidence of unlicensed practice is uncovered, the evidence must be compiled and presented to the Department of the Attorney General or the local district attorney's office for prosecution

3. **Unlicensed practice; criminal penalties.** Notwithstanding any other provision of law:

   A. A person who practices or represents to the public that the person is authorized to practice a profession or trade and intentionally, knowingly or recklessly fails to obtain a license as required by the laws relating to a board, commission or regulatory function identified in section 8001, subsection 38 or section 8001-A or intentionally, knowingly or recklessly practices or represents to the public that the person is authorized to practice after the license required by the laws relating to a board, commission or regulatory function identified in section 8001, subsection 38 or section 8001-A has expired or been suspended or revoked commits a Class E crime; and

   B. A person who practices or represents to the public that the person is authorized to practice a profession or trade and intentionally, knowingly or recklessly fails to obtain a license as required by the laws relating to a board, commission or regulatory function identified in section 8001, subsection 38 or section 8001-A or intentionally, knowingly or recklessly practices or represents to the public that the person is authorized to practice after the license required by the laws relating to a board, commission or regulatory function identified in section 8001, subsection 38 or section 8001-A has expired or been suspended or revoked when the person has a prior conviction under this subsection commits a Class D crime. Title 17-A, section 9-A governs the use of prior convictions when determining a sentence, except that, for purposes of this paragraph, the date of the prior conviction must precede the commission of the offense being enhanced by no more than 3 years.

4. **Unlicensed practice; civil penalties.** Any person who practices or represents to the public that the person is authorized to practice a profession or trade or engage in an activity that requires a license without first obtaining a license as required by the laws relating to a board, commission or regulatory function identified in section 8001, subsection 38 or section 8001-A or after the license has expired or has been suspended or revoked commits a civil violation punishable by a fine of not less than $1,000 but not more than $5,000 for each violation. An action under this subsection may be brought in District Court or, in combination with an action under subsection 5, in Superior Court.

5. **Unlicensed practice; injunctions.** The Attorney General may bring an action in Superior Court to enjoin any person from violating subsection 4, whether or not proceedings have been or may be instituted in District Court or whether criminal proceedings have been or may be instituted, and to restore to any person who has suffered any ascertainable loss by reason of that violation any money or personal or real property that may have been acquired by means of that violation and to compel the return of compensation received for engaging in that unlawful conduct.

A person who violates the terms of an injunction issued under this subsection shall pay to the State a fine of not more than $10,000 for each violation. In any action under this subsection, when a permanent injunction has been issued, the court may order the person against whom the permanent injunction is issued to pay to the General Fund the costs of the investigation of that person by the Attorney General and the costs of suit, including attorney's fees. In any action by the Attorney General brought against a person for violating the terms of an injunction issued under this subsection, the court may make the necessary orders or judgments to restore to any person who has suffered any ascertainable loss of money or personal or real property or to compel the return of compensation received by reason of such conduct found to be in violation of an injunction.

6. Unlicensed practice; private cause of action; repeal.

§8003-D. INVESTIGATIONS; ENFORCEMENT DUTIES; ASSESSMENTS

When there is a finding of a violation, a board or commission listed in section 8001-A may assess the licensed person or entity for all or part of the actual expenses incurred by the board, commission or its agents for investigations and enforcement duties performed.

"Actual expenses" include, but are not limited to, travel expenses and the proportionate part of the salaries and other expenses of investigators or inspectors, hourly costs of hearing officers, costs associated with record retrieval and the costs of transcribing or reproducing the administrative record.

The board or commission, as soon as feasible after finding a violation, shall give the licensee notice of the assessment. The licensee shall pay the assessment in the time specified by the board or commission, which may not be less than 30 days.

§8003-E. CITATIONS AND FINES

Any board or commission identified in section 8001, subsection 38 or section 8001-A or a regulatory function administered by the Office of Professional and Occupational Regulation identified in section 8001, subsection 38 may adopt by rule a list of violations for which citations may be issued by professional technical support staff. A violation may carry a fine not to exceed $200. Citations issued by employees of the Office of Professional and Occupational Regulation or an affiliated board must expressly inform the licensee that the licensee may pay the fine or request a hearing before the board or commission or the Office of Professional and Occupational Regulation with regard to a regulatory function identified in section 8001, subsection 38 administered by the office regarding the violation.

§8003-F. DISPOSITION OF FEES

All money received by the Office of Professional and Occupational Regulation on behalf of a board or commission listed in section 8001, subsection 38 or by the Office of Professional and Occupational Regulation to perform the regulatory functions listed in section 8001, subsection 38 must be paid to the Treasurer of State and credited to the account for that board, commission or regulatory function within the budget of the Office of Professional and Occupational Regulation.

Money received by the Office of Professional and Occupational Regulation on behalf of a board or commission listed in section 8001, subsection 38 or by the Office of Professional and Occupational Regulation to perform the regulatory functions listed in section 8001, subsection 38 must be used for the expenses of administering its statutory responsibilities, including, but not limited to, the costs of conducting investigations, taking testimony, procuring the attendance of witnesses, all legal proceedings initiated for enforcement and administering the office.

Any balance of these fees may not lapse but must be carried forward as a continuing account to be expended for the same purposes in the following fiscal years.

§8003-G. DUTY TO REQUIRE CERTAIN INFORMATION FROM APPLICANTS AND LICENSEES

The Office of Professional and Occupational Regulation, referred to in this subsection as "the office," including the licensing boards and commissions and regulatory functions within the office, shall require:

1. **Respond to inquiries**. All applicants for license renewal to respond to all inquiries set forth on renewal forms; and

2. **Report in writing**. All licensees and applicants for licensure to report in writing to the office no later than 10 days after the change or event, as the case may be:

   A. Change of name or address;

   B. Criminal conviction;

   C. Revocation, suspension or other disciplinary action taken in this or any other jurisdiction against any occupational or professional license held by the applicant or licensee; or

   D. Any material change in the conditions or qualifications set forth in the original application for licensure submitted to the office.

§8004. ANNUAL REPORTS

Notwithstanding any other provision of law, all annual reports or statements required of bureaus and offices within the department must be submitted to the commissioner not later than August 1st of each year and must summarize the operations and financial position of the bureau or office for the preceding fiscal year ending June 30th. After reviewing such reports and statements, the commissioner shall compile them into a report for submission to the Governor, together with such analysis as the Governor may direct.

§8004-A. LEGISLATIVE REPORTS

The Director of the Office of Professional and Occupational Regulation shall report annually to the joint standing committee of the Legislature having jurisdiction over professional licensing and registration on the status of licensing fees and fee caps.

§8005. COMPLIANCE WITH SUPPORT ORDERS; LICENSE QUALIFICATIONS AND CONDITIONS

In addition to other qualifications for licensure or registration and conditions for continuing eligibility to hold a license as prescribed by the various acts of bureaus, boards or commissions that compose or are affiliated with the department, applicants for licensure or registration, licensees renewing their licenses and existing licensees must also comply with the requirements of Title 19-A, section 2201.

§8005-A. LICENSEES NOT IN COMPLIANCE WITH COURT-ORDERED FINE, FEE OR RESTITUTION; LICENSE QUALIFICATIONS AND CONDITIONS

In addition to other qualifications for licensure or registration and conditions for continuing eligibility to hold a license as required by bureaus, boards and commissions within or affiliated with the department, applicants for licensure or registration, licensees renewing their licenses and existing licensees may not hold any such license when there has been a court-ordered suspension of that license as provided by Title 14, sections 3141 and 3142

§8006. LICENSEES NOT IN COMPLIANCE WITH COURT ORDER OF SUPPORT AND OTHER COURT ORDERS; ENFORCEMENT OF PARENTAL SUPPORT OBLIGATIONS AND SUSPENSIONS

1. Definitions. As used in this section, unless the context otherwise indicates, the following terms have the following meanings.

A. "Board" means any bureau, board or commission listed in section 8001 or 8001-A, other licensors that are affiliated with or are a part of the department and the Board of Overseers of the Bar.]

B. "Compliance with a support order" means that the support obligor has obtained or maintained health insurance coverage if required by a support order and is:

(1) No more than 60 days in arrears in making any of the following payments:

(a) Payments in full for current support;

(b) Periodic payments on a support arrearage pursuant to a written agreement with the Department of Health and Human Services; and

(c) Periodic payments as set forth in a support order; and

(2) No more than 30 days in arrears in making payments as described in subparagraph (1) if the obligor has been in arrears for more than 30 days in making payments as described in subparagraph (1) at least 2 times within the past 24 months.

C. "Support order" means a judgment, decree or order, whether temporary, final or subject to modification, issued by a court or an administrative agency of competent jurisdiction for the support and maintenance of a child, including a child who has attained the age of majority under the law of the issuing state, or a child and the parent with whom the child is living, that provides for monetary support, health care, arrearages or reimbursement and may include related costs and fees, interest and penalties, income withholding, attorney's fees and other relief.

D. "Court-ordered suspension" means a suspension by a court of the right of a licensee to hold a professional license based on the contempt procedures pursuant to Title 14, sections 3141 and 3142.]

2. Noncompliance with a support order. An applicant for the issuance or renewal of a license or an existing licensee regulated by a board who is not in compliance with a support order is subject to the requirements of Title 19-A, section 2201.

3. Court-ordered suspension. An applicant for the issuance or renewal of a license or an existing licensee regulated by a board who has not paid a court-ordered fine, court-appointed attorney's fees or court-ordered restitution is subject to court suspension of all licenses as provided in Title 14, sections 3141 and 3142.

§8007. BOARD MEMBER CANDIDATE INFORMATION

The Commissioner of Professional and Financial Regulation or the chief staff administrator for an occupational and professional regulatory board shall work with the Executive Department to prepare general information regarding the purpose of an occupational and professional regulatory board and the role, responsibility and perspective of a member of an occupational and professional regulatory board, including a public member. The material must also include information specific to the board for which the individual is a prospective member, including but not limited to the time commitment, remuneration and any other pertinent details.

This information must be provided to all new candidates for membership on an occupational and professional regulatory board and to members seeking reappointment in order to fully inform the candidate or member about the nature of the position. Prior to gubernatorial appointment or reappointment, the candidate or member shall sign a statement indicating that the candidate or member has read the material and is prepared to properly discharge the duties of a member of an occupational and professional regulatory board. Failure to sign this statement disqualifies the candidate or member for appointment or reappointment on a board.

§8008. PURPOSE OF OCCUPATIONAL AND PROFESSIONAL REGULATORY BOARDS

The sole purpose of an occupational and professional regulatory board is to protect the public health and welfare. A board carries out this purpose by ensuring that the public is served by competent and honest practitioners and by establishing minimum standards of proficiency in the regulated professions by examining, licensing, regulating and disciplining practitioners of those regulated professions. Other goals or objectives may not supersede this purpose.

§8009. STANDARDIZED TERMS

Notwithstanding any other provision of law, upon expiration of a professional or occupational licensing board member's term, that member serves until a successor is appointed. The successor's term commences at the expiration of the preceding term, regardless of the date of appointment. A vacancy occurring prior to the expiration of a specified term must be filled by appointment of a similarly qualified individual as a replacement. The replacement member serves for the remainder of the unexpired term, regardless of the date of appointment.

§8010. QUORUM; CHAIR

Notwithstanding any provision of law to the contrary, a majority of the members serving on a board or commission under section 8001, subsection 38 constitutes a quorum. The board or commission shall elect its chair.

§8011. VETERANS AND MILITARY SPOUSES

By January 1, 2014, each board, commission, office and agency within the department listed in section 8001 or affiliated with the department under section 8001-A shall adopt a process to facilitate qualified returning military veterans and qualified spouses of returning military veterans or of active duty service members to qualify for professional licenses granted by those boards, commissions, offices and agencies in an expeditious manner. For the purposes of this section, "returning military veteran" means a veteran of the Armed Forces of the United States who has been honorably discharged from active duty. Notwithstanding any other provision of law, the Director of the Office of Professional and Occupational Regulation and each licensing board within or affiliated with the department shall, upon presentation of satisfactory evidence by an applicant for professional or occupational licensure, accept education, training or service completed by the applicant as a member of the Armed Forces of the United States or Reserves of the United States Armed Forces, the national guard of any state, the military reserves of any state or the naval militia of any state toward the qualifications to receive the license.

1. **Endorsement.** The board, commission, office or agency may permit a returning military veteran or a spouse of a returning military veteran or of an active duty service member who holds a comparable license in another state to acquire a license by endorsement in this State for the

remainder of the term of the license from the other state or until a license is obtained in this State.

2. **Temporary license.** The board, commission, office or agency may permit a returning military veteran or a spouse of a returning military veteran or of an active duty service member who holds a comparable license in another state to obtain a temporary license in this State for a period of time necessary to obtain a license in this State.

3. **Acceptance of military credentials.** The board, commission, office or agency shall permit a returning military veteran whose military training qualifies the veteran for a license in a profession or occupation that requires a license in this State to acquire a temporary license until a license is issued.

4. **Continuing education requirements.** The board, commission, office or agency may allow a full or partial exemption from continuing education requirements for a returning military veteran or the spouse of a returning military veteran or of an active duty service member. Evidence of completion of continuing education requirements may be required for a subsequent license or renewal. A board, commission, office or agency shall provide that continuing education requirements may be met by comparable military training.

SELECTED RULES OPOR

Chapter 10: ESTABLISHMENT OF LICENSE FEES

Summary: This chapter establishes fees for professional and occupational licenses and registrations issued by the Office of Professional and Occupational Regulation.

1. Definitions

Unless the context otherwise indicates, the following words have the following meanings:

1. **3d party.** "3d party" refers to a fee for a standardized license examination that is paid directly by the applicant to the organization administering the examination or its designee.
2. **OPOR.** "OPOR" means the Office of Professional and Occupational Regulation.

2. Establishment of Fees; Effective Dates

OPOR shall charge the license and other fees indicated in §§ 3 and 5 below. For initial licenses, and for applications and examinations, the fees set out below shall become effective upon the effective date of this chapter. For renewal licenses, the fees set out below shall become effective with the first renewal cycle occurring on or after the effective date of this chapter.

The license and other fees of OPOR boards and regulatory functions not listed below are set by the statute and implementing rules governing the particular board or regulatory function.

3. Fees Applicable to All Boards and Regulatory Functions ... Listed in §4

Except as otherwise indicated, the fees listed in this section apply to all boards and regulatory functions listed in §5 below:

1. Photocopies ... No charge for first 7 pages, 25¢ for each page thereafter
2. Licensee register list on diskette or CD-ROM $25

4. Refunds

If an applicant applies for a license listed in §5 for which a separate application fee is charged, the license fee will be refunded if the license is denied. All other fees listed in §§ 3 and 5 are nonrefundable.

5. Fees to be Charged For Particular Occupational and Professional Licenses and Registrations and Related Fees

The following fees shall be charged for the licenses, registrations, permits and other services listed in subsections 1–40 below. For any given license or registration, the designated fee shall apply to both initial issuance and renewal unless otherwise indicated. The term of a license or registration ends on the uniform expiration or renewal date established for that license or registration by law.

35. Real Estate Commission

Real Estate Agency	2yr	$100
Real Estate Broker	2yr	$100
Associate Real Estate Broker	2yr	$100
Real Estate Sales Agent	limited 2yr	$100
Real Estate Sales Agent Extension	limited 1yr	$100
Inactive License	2yr	$100
Examination	NA	3d party
Continuing Education Course Application	NA	$50
Continuing Education Late Filing	NA	$100
Continuing Education Distance Education Course Application (per clock hour)	NA	$25
Continuing Education Individual Request	NA	$20
Pre-license Syllabus Application	NA	$80
Pre-license Late Filing	NA	$100
Record Modification (address, employer, name, etc)	NA	$20

Chapter 11: LATE RENEWALS

SUMMARY: This chapter establishes a uniform policy regarding the treatment of late renewals of licenses issued by the licensing boards and regulatory functions within the Office of Professional and Occupational Regulation ("OPO R")

Section 1. Applicability

This chapter applies to the OPOR licensing boards and regulatory functions enumerated in 10 MRSA &8001(38). For those programs, this chapter supersedes existing statutory and rule provisions dealing with the consequences of late renewal.

Section 2. Late Renewal Within 90 Days of Expiration

1. A licensee who applies for renewal after expiration of the license but within 90 days of expiration shall pay a late renewal fee of $50. The license will be issued as of the date of the late renewal and will not be retroactive to the expiration of the prior license.
2. The licensee is considered to have been unlicensed from the date of expiration to the date of late renewal.
3. A Licensee who applies for renewal within 90 days after expiration and pays the $50 late renewal fee will not be subject to disciplinary action by the licensing authority for unlicensed practice during the

period of nonlicensure. The licensee will remain subject to disciplinary action for all other violations.

Section 3. Late Renewal Beyond 90 Days of Expiration

A licensee who fails to renew within 90 days after expiration shall be subject to:

1. Applicable administrative and judicial penalties for all unlicensed practice that occurred subsequent to expiration; and
2. Applicable statutory provisions relating to late renewal.

Section 4. Notice

Licensees who fail to timely renew shall be notified of the consequences of late renewal as soon as practicable
after expiration.

Chapter 13: UNIFORM RULE FOR THE SUBSTANTIATION OF CONTINUING EDUCATION REQUIREMENTS

SUMMARY: This chapter establishes the substantiation of continuing education requirements for professional and occupational licensees and registrations issued by the Office of Professional and Occupational Regulation.

Section 1. Applicability

This chapter applies to all boards and regulatory functions with the Office of Professional and Occupational Regulation that require licensees to complete continuing education as a prerequisite to license renewal. This Chapter does not affect a board's authority to require or approve continuing education activities or to establish the number and nature of continuing education hours required for renewal.

Section 2. Certification of continuing education for renewal

At the time of application for renewal, each licensee must certify, on a form provided by the Office of Professional and Occupational Regulation, the number of continuing education hours completed during the preceding license term or during the continuing education period established in statute or by board rule. No additional information or continuing education documentation is required to be submitted at the time of renewal. However, the licensee must retain documentation of all continuing education activities as described in section 4 of this chapter.

Section 3. Verification of compliance by audit

Applicants for license renewal will be selected by the licensing board on a random basis for audit of continuing education compliance. In addition, an individual licensee may be selected for an audit as part of an investigation if there is reasonable cause to believe the licensee has provided a false certification concerning the completion of continuing education requirements. An audit may review the last two continuing education certifications submitted by the licensee. Licensees selected for audit will be notified to submit documentation of the continuing education activities that were certified by the licensee at the time of renewal. Continuing education hours that cannot be documented in accordance with the documentation requirements determined by the licensing board or that do not satisfy the criteria for continuing education contained in statute or board rule will be disallowed.

Section 4. Retention of Documentation

The licensee shall retain documentation of continuing education activities included in the most recent two continuing education certifications submitted by the licensee, including the current renewal period

About Walter Boomsma

Walter Boomsma's career as an educator/teacher began in the mid-seventies as part of a dealer development program for a national retailer. In 1985 he started his own consulting company specializing in individual and organizational development nationwide.

Walter says that it was perhaps fate that found him working with kids shortly after he "semi-retired" from a life on the road to Maine in 2002. His experiences with the kids led to his book "Small People—Big Brains: stories about simplicity, exploration, and wonder" released in 2013.

One chapter of his book is titled, "I'm Quitting Teaching." He quickly admits he's not retiring, but "I've actually been giving up teaching for a quite a few years now... I'm constantly doing it differently because teaching is really about learning. I believe learning should be as much fun as possible. When it's not fun, it should at least be rewarding." Maybe that's why he gives stickers—not just to the kindergarteners, but to adults as well.

Walter has been teaching real estate courses for nearly fifteen years. He is a licensed real estate broker associated with Mallett Real Estate in Dover Foxcroft, Maine.

In addition to offering learning opportunities with several adult education programs, "Mr. Boomsma" is also an elementary school substitute teacher, grades kindergarten through six.

http://abbotvillagepress.com

For more information about courses and learning opportunities read "Brain Leaks and Musings" at http://wboomsma.com.

Books published by Abbot Village Press

Abbot Village Press
Books, Blogs & Education with purpose

Small People – Big Brains: Stories About Simplicity, Exploration, and Wonder

In this book, Mr. Boomsma shares some of his experiences with kids over the past decade as a volunteer and, most recently, substitute elementary school teacher. Many of these short stories will make you laugh. Some will make you cry. All will make you think. The title of the book comes from an encounter with a young fellow who was firmly convinced that his difficulties at school were the result of his brain being too small. The stories, however, prove that these small people really do have big brains. They just haven't discovered and fully learned how to use them yet.

Exploring Traditions—Celebrating the Grange Way of Life

"These essays by Walter Boomsma unpack the teachings of the Grange and relate them to today's world and our everyday lives," writes Betsy Huber, National Master (President) of the Grange. Many people, including Grange members themselves, seem to be wondering about the relevance of this 150-year-old organization in modern society. They may find some answers in Exploring Traditions—Celebrating the Grange Way of Life, a series of essays encouraging readers to understand the basis of Grange ritual and tradition. This is not a "guide to the Grange," it truly is an exploration of some of the words and actions found in the Grange ritual and tradition. Included are the Grange Mission Statement and Declaration of purposes, allowing readers to take away from the book a new and deeper understanding of the Grange—not merely as an historical organization, but also an organization that teaches a way of life that aligns us with nature and creates community.

Betsy Huber, Master (President), The National Grange

Mr. Boomsma's Substitute Teacher Workbook

This workbook was developed for use in "Mr. Boomsma's Substitute Teacher Workshop" and, as such may appear to be missing content if viewed without participating. However, there is plenty of standalone information and valuable resources. It should further be noted that some of the information such as the process for fingerprinting and background checks is specific to the State of Maine. Regulations and processes may differ widely among states and school districts. The Substitute Teacher Workshop is currently offered by three Adult Education Programs. Additional information is available at http://wboomsma.com.

Maine Real Estate Law and Rule Handbook
Edited by Walter Boomsma and produced with the goal of making it student friendly, this handbook has application to all three licensing courses currently offered in Maine: Sales Agent, Associate Broker, and Designated Broker as well as many continuing education programs. In addition, real estate licensees and companies will find the handbook a handy guide to the daily practice of real estate brokerage in Maine.

Future Release: **Words for Thirds Grange Dictionary Program Handbook**
The Dictionary Project is a powerful program designed to provide students with their own personal dictionary. This handbook will explore how to start and maximize the benefits of implementing a local program. While the emphasis is on a Grange Program, the techniques and information can be adopted to any civic or community organization that wants to empower students. Strategies for implementation, fundraising suggests, presentation outlines, and sample media advisories and press releases are included. Much of the material is based on the successful program started over ten years ago by Valley Grange. The program has expanded to include four school districts and has distributed over 3,000 dictionaries to date

Future Release: **Conversations with Substitute Teachers (working title)**
Conversations about many of the unique challenges substitute teachers face and how to meet those challenges without tearing your hair out!

- **Author's online store**:

  https://squareup.com/market/abbot-village-press

· **Author's Amazon Page**:

  https://www.amazon.com/Walter-Boomsma/

- **Barnes and Noble online:**

  https://www.barnesandnoble.com/

  or by special order at Barnes and Noble stores.

www.ingramcontent.com/pod-product-compliance
Lightning Source LLC
Chambersburg PA
CBHW071237020426
42333CB00015B/1518